A Book of One's Own

A Book of One's Own

DEVELOPING LITERACY THROUGH MAKING BOOKS

Paul Johnson

Graphic illustrator: Jayne Restall

Hodder & Stoughton

LONDON SYDNEY AUCKLAND TORONTO

To those whose books comprise this book

British Library Cataloguing in Publication Data

Johnson, Paul
  A book of one's own.
  1. Books. Design
  I. Title
  686

  ISBN 0 340 53352 8

First published 1990

Typeset by Gecko Limited, Bicester, Oxon
*Printed in Hong Kong for the educational publishi 1g division of Hodder
and Stoughton Ltd, Mill Road, Dunton Green, Sevenoaks, Kent by
Colorcraft Ltd, Hong Kong.*

Contents

Introduction

On a July morning in 1984 I knew, quite suddenly, the time had come for me to make books. I had grown up in a tiny house wallpapered with them, for my father spent every penny of his pocket money adding to his collection. A great treat would be for him to take one down from the shelves and cerimoniously show me the pictures they contained. So it was that I fell in love with books, not only for their content but as objects to be touched, held and possessed. They were to me (and still are) intimate companions of immeasurable worth. As I write I look up to the shelves of books before me and marvel at the variety of their size, shape and design. Each one is a sentence in my autobiography, stepping stones to a wider concept of who I am.

After breakfast on that July morning I took a book to pieces to see how it was made and then started to make one myself. Shortly afterwards I went to teach at the State University of San Francisco and found to my delight that San Francisco was a Mecca for book artists of every kind brought together by the Pacific Center for the Book Arts. I came home to England so bursting with ideas for books that I haven't stopped making them since.

Soon, I was invited to schools to make books with children. I seized upon this in order to share with children the delight of self-made books and it is this experience which comprises the body of this book.

In this depersonalised world we seek ways of making things 'our own'. Children cover their exercise books with wallpaper to personalise them; failing that, covers are decorated with patterns or graffiti to make them less formal. But to make a book of one's own is to have found an enrichment of life and a furthering of one's identity. Teachers who have made books with children know that when a book is part of a writing project, interest in, and devotion to, the acquisition of language skills increases phenomenally. Excellence in writing becomes a self-imposed objective, because the self-made book which houses the text is a treasured item. So intimately valuable are these books to children that I have to rely, almost exclusively, on photographs and slide records, because the owners will not part with them. (On a darker note they become irresistible to others also. Some half dozen books illustrated here were stolen from an exhibition.) But teachers must experience the magic of making books too, if genuine enthusiasm for book art is to be communicated to children.

Books can be about, or of, anything. There is no part of the curriculum that cannot find meaning in the book form. However, for the purposes of this book an accent has been placed on self-made story books because children have a special relationship with story imagery and acquire most language skills through it in the early years. Hardly any specialist equipment is necessary. A sharp knife, a long steel ruler, a bookbinder's awl, darning needles (and, if possible, a cutting mat) are all that is required. Indeed for several of the books described here only a piece of paper and a pair of scissors are needed. This may prompt the question 'What is a book?' This is a dialectical question to which I do not intend to address myself, except to say that I conceptualise any form of communication which is in some way 'hinged', and therefore capable of opening and closing as a 'book'. Every time one attempts to make a book one is redefining the book concept. It is this spirit of exploration, of questioning and adapting old, and inventing new, ways of making books that lies at the heart of this book.

In recent times there has been an emphasis on children developing sound academic and technical skills: it is firmly believed that they should acquire the ability to interrelate forms of practical experience, to question, synthesize, test, speculate and learn to evaluate their efforts. The attention that the National Curriculum has directed towards cross-curricular activities addresses these concerns. There is probably no more efficient way for teachers to implement these issues than through the book arts which integrate so many basic and fundamental skills, as this book will show. But parallel to these pragmatic pursuits in education has been a growing awareness that there is more to schooling than formal learning as a preparation for industrial careers and the enterprise culture. In each one of us is a spiritual centre, a realm of feeling, a need to create beauty, and a primordial instinct to reflect and express. Here again, the self-made book comes into its own as a vehicle of identifying that which is most precious to us, a means of self-discovery in one of the most personal ways possible.

I have not gone out of my way to reproduce 'excellent' examples of children's books. Where exemplary work has been produced as part of a scheme these have sometimes been used, but unspectacular work is represented too. I have tried to show a very average mix for, in many cases, a marked achievement for a child is not echoed in the work produced – a few scribbled words on a folded page may represent a milestone of development. This is an anthology of children's books reflecting all stages of cognitive, emotional and manipulative growth. Each book 'tells a story' – a hidden story about the author which is told in the *way* the book is conceived, produced, presented; and therein lies 'a mystery of meaning', as one teacher put it. This will remain a mystery for all except those most intimately involved with the children concerned.

One word of warning: there is always the danger that the book-creating ideas disseminated here will be used as novelty, one-off experiences for children. This would be to bypass the dynamic role of book art, developmentally, in children's acquisition of fundamental skills of learning. The books here illustrate children's statements at all stages from nursery to top junior. It is for teachers to devise sequential schemes of work in progressive stages of skill mastery to reap the benefits of book art.

There is much that is missing from this book – multicultural, gender and special needs aspects of book art, for example – but I hope the reader will forgive me for focusing attention on the universality of the genre and its application to every child. These important areas will, I am sure, find their way into later book art publications.

As for children's language development in general, this is so vast and well documented that my contribution is limited to two areas: (*i*) the making of improvised stories with children, and (*ii*) how the book concept itself stimulates writing. What has come to be known as 'process writing' – drafting, conferencing, editing and publishing – is a widely discussed approach to children's writing which I endorse but omit from my text to avoid repetition. Those not familiar with the technique and its manifestations should refer to the book list section and assimilate these ideas in conjunction with the story book ideas proposed here.

In this context, children are often encouraged to write with a specific audience in mind. However, sometimes it may be preferable for children to produce a story first and then to decide for whom it is suitable. It is up to the teacher to decide whether or not this is a technique for developing 'styles' of writing they wish to pursue.

Handwriting, another constituent part of book art, receives scant attention here. Judging by the vast range of books on calligraphy available, it is in the ascendant, both in and out of education.

Although a radical, I am also a conservative, and correct spelling, punctuation, syntax and good sentence construction have a beauty of another kind when it comes to books. The hand-made, heart-felt, spirit-moved, mind-formed book *is* the best stimulus for all these 'traditional' skills because children want to give of their best in them. And if we demand the best of which each child is capable, we must give them the best. There is a myth that good cartridge paper is expensive. At the time of writing, a book from one piece of A2 quality cartridge can be made for 3p; or put another way, a class of thirty or more pupils can make a book each for around £1.00. If we give our children torn and faded sugar paper or gossamer thin newsprint it is fatuous to expect a commitment from them. I have always found, the better the paper, the *greater* the commitment.

In the chapters that follow I begin by looking at 'The Book' as a work of art. In my teaching of book art I try to show children that they are part of a great tradition, that our culture has its roots in communication through books; that the spirit of what is communicated is through the design, quality of paper, letter face, excellence of illustration and binding.

Next I turn my attention to the heart of the book concept for children – story making itself – and to a reappraisal of the oral tradition of story making through improvisation. (The skills of oral communication are given priority in the National Curriculum.) This is developed in the simplest of all books, the concertina. Then I explore the concepts that 'the book' can stimulate, direct and foster what goes on inside them. This hypothesis is tested through a series of projects involving books made from one single sheet of paper. Most of these projects were undertaken at Beaver Road Primary School, in Manchester, and my thanks go to the staff for allowing me to try out my ideas on their children.

I go on to examine books made by infants, embracing both traditional and experimental styles, and am indebted to Beryl Edwards for the illuminating work of her children illustrated here. A section on nursery books is also included.

Attention is then focused on a classroom collaborative book embracing many styles of writing. This reflects the concern of the National Curriculum for children acquiring skills in many uses of written language. A chapter including group story books, the side-binding technique and the European method follows. The final two sections look briefly at the use of computers in book art and thematic class books.

I would like to thank the staff and children of Brookburn Primary School, Chorlton, Manchester and Queens Road Primary School, Stockport who allowed me to work so freely amongst them; and also to three schools whose children's work are represented here: Broadheath Primary School, Trafford; Mill Hill Primary School, Oldham; and Hey with Zion Primary School, Oldham.

Most importantly, I want those who read this book to be stimulated to not only make their own books, but *invent* their own.

A book is anything you want it to be.

1 The book as art

I can just about remember my first book. Well, it wasn't really a book, more a bound folder and I was ten. All the measurements had been put on the black-board and we had the necessary tools and materials. Recall does not furnish me with the length of time it took to make, but I can see in my mind's eye a warped, dark brown object with glue oozing out of it. I think it was probably one of the most unpleasant things I have ever held, and when I took it to the class teacher's desk to get my mark he said in despair, 'Well, one thing's for certain: you'll never make an artist.'

I don't think that at any time at school reasons were given why one should make craft objects other than that they were 'useful'. Traditional bookbinding as practised in many schools before, during and after the war, was seen as an adaptation of a masterly skill to a child's level. One simply practised well-defined skills with known outcomes. From the early sixties the traditional crafts like bookbinding, basketry and crochet were systematically dropped from the curriculum. The growing popularity of child-centred education and open-plan schools pioneered a new philosophy of education which promoted self-discovery as the prime means of learning. Clearly, to such a spirit of adventure, traditional bookbinding appeared grotesquely passé.

In my first teaching appointment in 1964 the bookbinding presses were used as potted plant stands. But attitudes in education are cyclical. Design and technology are now highlighted in the National Curriculum. Practical skills which can be adapted to other processes and ends are encouraged. Schools are seen as training grounds for creative invention and entrepreneurial flair. If goods are to sell they must be attractively designed and packaged. It is in the making of books that these seeds are planted. Children need imaginative teaching to enhance the basic technical skills of bookbinding with the innovative challenge of book-form inventing. One of the questions I put to children is 'What makes a book cover attractive?' – arrangement of shapes, colour relationships, lettering, eye-catching artwork? Using the richness of the best of published story books to stimulate (but not indoctrinate) children's aesthetic sensitivity, I encourage them to plan designs for their own books.

The spirit of Technology in the National Curriculum is for children to be engaged in the generation of design proposals and to be personally involved in the planning and making stages:

'Pupils' ability to respond effectively to new needs and opportunities by the design and making of original or better products will be important to them personally, but it will also be an essential condition for the future prosperity of our business-industry.'

In this design technology context, children are responsible for the whole book design task – layout, lettering, handwriting/computer letterface, diagrams, charts, binding style and method. (In the programme of study for level 1, it is stated that children should be taught to recognise that materials and components can be linked in various ways to make movement, for example hinges. The books, of course, especially the experimental books suggested here, *are* 'mechanisms' – for they are folded, lifted and manipulated in most ingenious ways.)

One has only to visit either the British Museum or the Victoria and Albert Museum to see the status of 'the book' as a work of art. Unitl the late Middle Ages, when printing changed the whole concept, the book was a venerated and treasured object of great spiritual and mercenary value. Real gold was applied to every page, book covers were encrusted with precious stones and ivory. Artists and scribes would spend years on one illuminated book of the Gospels. Every page was a singular work of art and would be highly decorated so that the eye would be held from cover to cover, not only by what was written but *how* it was presented. These

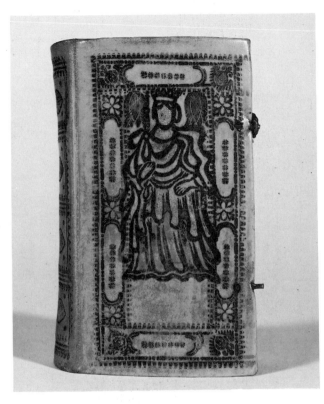

Gold-tooled white velum cover, Germany 1707 (Reproduced with permission of British Library)

Page from The Koran, *Egypt, 14th century (Reproduced with permission of British Library)*

attitudes were universal in the literate world and in countries where printing was later in arriving, like the Middle East, India and Japan, the book as a one-off object of great beauty prevailed as a possession of the very highest status. The book also unifies art and language, for both forms exist one inside the other. One sees the art through the writing and the writing through the art. The illustrations support and amplify the text and, reciprocally, the text gives the artist subject-matter on which to liberate his visual imagination. The binder, in no less a role than the scribe and illustrator, bound these works of art in covers designed with breathtaking beauty.

When teaching book art I use reproductions of, for example, *The Book of Kells* to show children that each page of writing, illustration (or a combination of the two) should be carefully designed. The turning of the pages of their books should excite the eye with anticipation.

It is only comparatively recently that, in the West at least, the one-off book has found a revival of interest. A handful of galleries specialise in 'artists' books' which are usually experimental in nature and explore paper and book concepts. In the category of fine binding experiments, Philip Smith is surely a master, producing designs in leather of great beauty, some more like sculptures than conventional ideas of what constitutes a book cover. These too, I show to children, either in reproduction or, wherever possible, the real object.

Nasa Takina's *The book that got all mixed up inside* is a book cut to pieces and rearranged. Children are fascinated by this and are at liberty to change the arrangement of pages. I think it unlikely that they will be influenced by it, but it is essential that they are aware of what is happening in the world of books at large.

Like so many other areas, more changes have taken place in the book concept in the last thirty years than in the previous three hundred. This is a pluralistic society, a cultural environment in which inspired individuals rather than collective ideologies symbolise the spirit of the times. There are as many kinds of books as there are individuals producing them. The feeling of individuality which is so much part of the book concept is further underlined by the personal, intimate ownership of one's own book. As I have already said, children become very attached to their books, and although some of the projects recorded here are joint, collaborative efforts, I respect the desire of children to be personally responsible for the *whole* of their books – story, artwork, presentation and binding. Even children who declare that they 'can't draw' still prefer to do their own illustrations in many cases.

The innovation of printing did not kill the

Hand embossed box by Natalie d'Arbeloff for the book The Word Accomplished *by A.B. Christoper*

The Silmarillion *(R.R. Tolkien) binding in tower container by Philip Smith (Heller Collection, London)*

The book that got all mixed up inside, *Nasa Takina*

spirit of the one-off book completely. Personal journals embodying writing and illustration have long been a source of identification for artists/writers. It is not just a sketch book which primarily contains drawings, but a dialogue between word and image. (Van Gogh gives a good example of this in his drawing/notebooks.) My most treasured possessions are letters and small improvised

Brown paper bag and plastic carrier bag books (student)

book packages containing paintings, collages and words sent to me by the special people in my life. With one person in particular I have had a postal relationship of this kind for several years. It is a very private exchange and we speak to each other as much through colour and line as with words.

The greatness of William Blake's work lies in his synthesis of verbal and visual form. I often think how wrong it is to print his poems in typeface when it is the very drawing of his letter shapes and adjoining allegorical material in which he says so much. Indeed, one of the misfortunes of printing is that it has given rise to doubts about the appropriateness of handwriting as a viable means of communication. The printed page carries more weight than the handwritten one. Writers and poets only see themselves as successful 'when in print'; it is the typeset

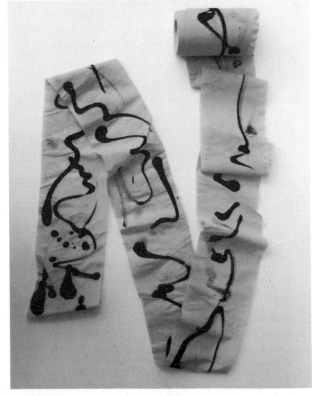

Books with collage covers (student)

Toilet paper 'scroll' book (student)

serif letters that give stature and authority to their work. Wherever possible I show children facsimile published material (my favourite is Richard Doyle's *Journal of 1840* (Bartholomew, Edinburgh 1980)) so they can appreciate how beautiful a page of handwriting and drawing can be. One of the pleasures I find in interviewing students for the Manchester Polytechnic PGCE Art and Design course is in going through their journals and notebooks. Usually these are far more interesting, lively and original than their mounted artwork and say infinitely more about them. I recently interviewed a student who had made a visual journal of her home, drawing and writing about virtually every object around her. My own journals are so much part of me that I know my life would be weakened without them.

Computerised word processors have revolutionised the visual orientation of writing, and one must endorse the attention paid to it by the National Curriculum. To ignore its potential in language development would be folly, and to disregard its role in our developing technological society, suicidal. But the type processed word image will always be alien to that part of communication which is demonstrably personal.

A great Japanese philosopher and calligrapher defined writing as a 'dance for the hand'. Words dance across the page in a form of drawing – 'the art of handwriting'. When empathy exists between writer and the penned word, something quite magical is always on the cards because the coordinated mind/eye/hand is the greatest computer of them all. Writing should be a joy, a harmony of feelings and ideas manifested as shapes sprung into life on a white stage. Finding our style of writing is a symbol of our humanity.

An allied trend to the personalised one-off book is for schools to publish their children's books by typing stories, adding line drawings and then using the school photocopier to 'run them off'. The whole is then stapled through a card cover designed by the pupil concerned. This is an excellent way of approaching book

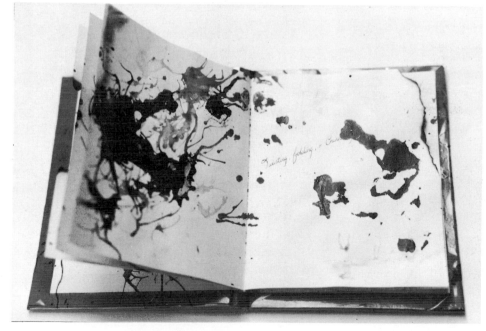

Twisting and folding book (student)

Paper cut-out book (student)

Extract from Richard Doyle's journal (Reproduced with permission of the British Library)

brown at half past one. We past over Primrose hill just as the sun was setting. We arrived at M Bassetts at eight and tea being just over the circumstance added considerably to our joy to think that we should have nearly lost our tea a second time We spent a very pleasant evening M Selous came and walked a part of the way home with us, and not being able to get a coach, a cab was hailed and all the party but James and I stuffed into it. We set off at a quick trot and reached home a few minutes after the vehicle having met with nothing on the road beyond drunken men at intervals

THURSDAY. 14. Tutor came at 12 lol Shultze says he wont go till January The Dancing Envelope has failed in the printing and I have got to do it over again. I would a great deal sooner do anything as large as a Tournament than the size of the envelopes on transfer paper.

FRIDAY. Doing envelopes all day in the evening went with Ruff to the Serpentine

Saturday. Papa made an appointment to with the lol to Canterbury to day. He said he would be here at half past ten and Papa had been waiting

CLARKE BOOKSELLER & STATIONER

FINCH LANE.

102

art, but one which needs a whole book dedicated to it.

The NCC English statutory order at key stage 1 states that pupils should undertake work in producing invitations, greeting cards and posters, and suggests finished pieces in the form of newspapers, magazines and books. Much of this reflects the growing concern for children's language development through writing disseminated by the National Writing Project. There is a marked practical approach to writing today: it is felt that children should be able to communicate in many styles, not only narrative writing as in storytelling, but in descriptive writing, reporting and letter writing. Informational and transactional styles need to be understood too.

The NCC Technology statutory orders, attainment target 2 'Generating a design' (Level 4), gives as an example children keeping records containing sketches, pictures, stimulus materials or notes.

All in all the *modus operandi* is for children to be able to interrelate a wide range of visual communication strategies – writing in many forms, diagrams, captioned pictures and graphic illustrations.

The book concept has a unique part to play in all these developments. The remarkable thing is that the story book can do justice to all of them. Chapter 6 'A book of many styles' shows the work of a year four class combining poster design, newspaper article writing, broadcasting, reporting, letter writing,

writing, artwork, design and lettering, all within a story framework. The artwork required as much care and attention as the written tasks. If approached with insight, children's illustration should not only be a product of the imagination but a statement of the observed world; as clear and revealing a form of communication as writing.

Jung's legacy to all of us was to show the universality of our identity through mythological images. He said that we were of an immense age, carrying our 'symbolic life' through time and eternity. It is through story telling, story-picture making and poetry that the soul finds its voice in the shaping of moral and ethical concepts; that our life-plans are given substance and our relationships with others infused with direction. But Jung was eager to argue that the archetypes of the collective unconscious manifest themselves in ever-changing ways. Creative expression keeps the evolving mythology alive. Without expression we have a stereotypical rhetoric and, without mythology, we, in a psychological sense, lose ourselves. The book form is itself a mythological experience, a symbolic journey revealing the transformative vision of self-renewal.

One has only to visit a bookshop to see the emphasis publishers place on children's literature. If the development of language skills depends significantly on reading, then story books hold the key to a literate nation. I had doubts at first that children would compare their own books with those published in the school library, but I was delighted to find that no child ever did this. They seemed to identify so closely with their own books that nothing could distract them.

Children's expectations of purchased books are very high. The stories have to be exciting and engaging, the artwork compelling, the book design colourful and attractive. But more especially these days, children's books are more experimental in concept and construction, leaving adult books far behind. The implication for radical curriculum design is that the books our children are encouraged to make must be at least as exciting as ones they can buy.

In the preparatory stages it seemed important that the verbal and visual content, binding method and presentation of children's self-made books should be interrelated. I wanted them to see the whole of it as if it was one. The weakness of traditional bookbinding for schools lies in the title. It is the binding as a technique that matters, not 'the book' as an integrated concept. The way we conceive a book from binding method to size, shape and colour of pages (indeed the surface texture of the paper and its aroma) affects the way we internalise the book's contents. Just as primary red appears differently on a cobalt background than on an orange one, so the way we *perceive* words and pictures is conditioned by the form the book takes.

The unifying effect of book art, embracing so much, has a great deal to commend to cross-curriculum lesson planning. But it has its dangers. It would be wrong to suppose that every literary form is best suited to book presentation. To bind essays and forms of descriptive writing in a folder may be a better method. Artwork in books has its drawbacks, too. Books are usually small; their compactness is part of their meaning; therefore the pictorial forms in them are restricted in size. This denies children the opportunity to work large with paint, pencil or collage. Book-size artwork may well inhibit the freedom good art teaching is trying to encourage. Book art projects need to be supportive to, rather than replacements of, children learning through writing and art.

The influence of Robin Tanner, the father of children's book art, is widespread. Through his pioneering work over fifty years ago, excellence of design, handwriting, illustration and, of course, bookbinding, opened up a whole new vista for children.

In their book *Children Making Books* Leslie Bennett and Jack Simmons (ALC Black, London 1978) continued his pioneering work and provide an excellent reference book on more traditional bookbinding techniques. This book, however, takes a different starting point from theirs, and it is important to indicate that the methods I describe here are not necessarily traditionally accepted ways of bookbinding. I tend to take all manner of short-cuts, to strip procedures down to their base essentials in order to simplify a sophisticated and complex craft. Children, I found, demanded fast ways of working and whilst it is important for them to master skills, it is equally important that their interest and enthusiasm is not thwarted by laborious processes.

The scope of the book genre is vast. We see the evolution of man symbolised in all its changing forms. And if the subject is to be done justice in the curriculum, then paper-making, marbling, block printing should be included. The area of illustration is another aspect on which little has been written for teachers. In status terms, illustration falls below that of the fine arts, which is a nonsense, as some of the great illustrators are every bit as accomplished as their fine art opposites. Illustration also stands in second place to the story it accompanies. Look at any chidren's story book and you will see that the writer's name is above that of the illustrator. This is another nonsense, for the two should complement each other on equal terms. But the fact remains. So to avoid children undervaluing their illustrations I prefer to call them 'story art' or 'story pictures' in an attempt to redress the balance.

'Creative' and self-titled 'uncreative' teachers alike must not feel that superhuman skills are necessary for them to involve children in making books. It is impossible for me to describe the joy they will find when this happens, or the richness to be found in making a book oneself and not just 'getting the children to do it'. I run evening in-service courses for teachers regularly. Whenever we have made books the caretaker has actually had to throw us out on more than one occasion. Books are infectious.

2 *Story making for story books*

A great deal has been written about stimulating children to write 'creatively'. In the best of all possible worlds, expression would flow out of us, for as 'compulsive communicators' the need to externalise feelings through art of one sort or another would be intuitive. Sadly this is not so; the intuition of the infant spontaneously learning through play rarely finds a fruitful manifestation in adult life. Most teachers and older children are remedials in this context, for neither group feels confident in making creative statements. Yet the primary teacher has responsibility for 'creative writing' – often a frightening challenge. But there is a paradox. On the one hand, teachers are directed professionally towards creative writing and, on the other, away from it. In these reactionary times, creative writing comes under daily attack by those who see it as a dangerously permissive and subversive activity. A return to 'orthodoxy' is called for. But what is this orthodoxy? Not even the most practical uses of language – like writing a washing machine maintenance manual – can be conceived without the application of creative thought. The choice of words, the ability to condense complex concepts into easily understood descriptions, to define clearly yet accurately, calls for an imaginative intelligence on the part of the writer. Moreover, expressive writing is no less

'practical' than technical or transactional writing. Describing the idiosyncracies and mannerisms of people, their homes and places of work – whether it be reportage or fictional in nature – requires the ability to use language in structured, logical ways. There isn't one kind of sentence structure for fact and another for fantasy; both attend to the laws governing syntax and grammar. To read a page of Roald Dahl is to witness a master of English language at work. It would be hard to find any page of technical writing that uses such a wide vocabulary and variety of verbal compositional styles or clarity of description. Story writing is language in its highest form. But there is another justification for expressive writing in the curriculum – the externalisation and 'imagizing' of the hidden world of the unconscious. Not all may sympathise with Jung's 'collective unconscious', but no teacher can fail to recognise the immediacy with which children relate to the fantasy world of story telling. I believe that the handling of archetypes through children making their own stories is fundamental to the growth of the young. In the pages which follow this world of the inner being is brought to the surface. Through it, children view and review their attitudes and responses to experience, formulate moral and ethical values and explore the development and resolution of ideas. I don't intend to address myself to

children's story writing, only to the ways in which it fits the present context – children's self-made written and bound books. I describe my own approach to story stimulation, and it is for teachers to adapt this to their own methods. I am an incurable eclectic, appropriating everything I experience to my own use, absorbing other people's ideas into my own working practices.

Unlocking the imagination

Some doors into the imagination open easily, and some do not. But most are penetrable, providing the appropriate stimulation is applied. **The rusty door** – This kind of door, by far the most common, does not yield easily. It is fastened by misuse and needs constant oiling of hinges. It is typified by children being given ideas for a story, none of which are taken up and fed inwardly. So much care must be taken here for crafted means of entry are needed. To scrape away too rigorously (*'Now I want us to think out all the furnishings inside the underground castle. John you tell us all about the pictures on the walls, and Mary you tell us all about the things on the mantelpiece . . .'*) can damage the door itself, making entry even harder. Children can so easily be frightened by not being able to 'think of something', to be terrorised into nonparticipation, by insistence. Most destructive of all is the attempt to destroy the door with a hammer blow (*'What an unimaginative lot you all are. Now come on, Peter, surely you can think of something?'*) So much depends upon the rapport between teacher and taught. Children must feel at ease with the person who is conducting the story. An analogy with the orchestral conductor is a good one here, for he does not make the music himself but produces it from the players. The atmosphere must be relaxed, for tension caused by fear of what is to be expected of one is counter-productive. The class teacher has the advantage of oiling the door slowly and consistently. A careful, yet convivial daily story sequence improvisation can do much to facilitate a smoothly opening door to the imagination. The daily 'diary' ritual of the early classroom in which children describe the previous day's experiences and the next day's expectations, is a good preparation for story telling because it exercises the capacity to release words into the air. The gradual growing confidence engendered by children talking aloud is perhaps the best way of all of opening the imagination to the world, for words come direct without the intervention of writing. This accumulative dialogue has a force that cannot be overestimated and from which the greatest fruits of expression can be realised. Like learning to play the piano, it is the daily discipline of practice that lays the foundation of accomplishment. Doors which seem to be well and truly impassable may not be so.

Children can fly through the keyhole, and so reach inside themselves, without touching the door. This was the case with a girl I once taught who in the oral story making time said nothing yet her written story was full of invention. Oracy is important, but children are on so many different rungs of so many ladders, and climbing is an irregular business. Only the knowledge of individual children can enable the teacher as a story vessel to prod or to leave well alone. Some children, bored by school, become lazy and need a rigorous mental massage, whilst others, of an introverted nature, need another kind of coaxing. There are the natural extroverts, those with limited vocabularies or communication problems, the remedials and high attainers, and all of these bring to the story improvisation an inconsistency. It is the technique of the story-shaper to harmonise all these divergencies of input into a synthesised whole.

The well-oiled door – In nearly every story-making group I encounter, there is at least one child who is generally regarded as 'good' at telling stories by teachers and peers alike. The problem here is to suppress the monologue so that group interaction can take place. It is so easy to let the story grow in an almost solo or duo way, but it does nothing to unify the group. Of course spontaneity of this kind should be encouraged but in a controlled way. David, a pupil at Queen's Road Primary, was able to produce well-formed images at will. I used to fall back on him when we reached a

sticking point in the story and this would point us in a new direction. In this way he became a kind of associate conductor, an assistant to me when the need arose. (I think he found real confidence in this didactic role.)

Behind this main door between the inner and outer realities lie other doors. One door is marked **Popular Imagery**. Children who open this door inside them find celebrities lined up like cardboard cutouts. When I start a story with the words 'Give me a person . . .' or during a story I say 'And who was inside the flying refrigerator?', I nearly always get as a response a popular TV personality, the Prime Minister or the President of the USA. These are dead-enders in story telling, for even if one could extract some novel or inventive facet from personalities, they contain too much media overkill to be any use.

Ironically, larger-than-life images give off less potential than a pebble or a plate of mashed potatoes. The fewer the well-formed components of an image, the more the imagination can do with it. Often children will give 'Mickey Mouse' or some Saturday morning children's TV super hero as thematic material. Whilst these are from the realm of fantasy and so nearer to the unconscious domain, they are loaded with stereotype imagery. Now this imagery is often archetypal. It is what lies in the strata above the primordial commonality that is regurgitated in children's story making. The names of planets, spaceship captains and cartoon personalities creep into the improvisation and twist it into a prescribed formula. Just one interjection of 'Donald Duck' into an evolving story can disturb the delicate process of invention. Sometimes, when story making with children, it takes all the imaginative resources I have to steer away from the popular image. In a society in which children spend more time watching television than almost any other pursuit, the images on the screen become endemic. Like a virus, it attacks the imagination's own way of protecting itself. In both verbal and visual imagery these stereotypes have to be peeled off, and the child's capacity to create personality on archetypal forms invigorated.

One way I have of doing this is to accept the stereotype by saying, 'Well, yes, the Prime Minister was there, but who else?' Sometimes another stereotype follows, 'OK so next to the Prime Minister was the President of the United States of America, but . . .' Something has to happen here and happen quickly or we will go on collecting a stream of international figures from the Pope to Miss World, which will kill the story dead in its tracks. So what I say at this point is something like, 'But on the ground behind them lay a sealed envelope and inside was . . .?'

This kind of a twist away from the popular imagery is often all that is needed to get a story moving again. However, sometimes it can still stick and so drastic measures need to be taken: 'Inside the envelope was something that no one had ever seen before . . . it was round . . . and soft . . . and made music . . .'

With carefully orchestrated plot development firmly in the fantasy mode, the story can now proceed.

Another obstacle to expressive intervention is the door marked **Common Place Imagery**. Through this door children find forms of the immediate and near present: *the classroom* – class teacher, class gerbil; *the home environment* – my pet rabbit, bicycle, holiday places; *hobbies* – football, computer games. Stories revolve around supermarkets. If someone is ill, they have AIDS. If they go somewhere, it is Wembley or Butlins.

There is nothing 'wrong' with any of these, but if any real invention is to take place the story must rise above the ordinary and prosaic, to find the extraordinary in the ordinary. The craft of writing is essentially taking the familiar and illuminating it so that we see it in a new light – in great writing – as for the first time. In story making, supermarkets can be full of magic sauce bottles or jars of condensed planets; the classroom can be mysteriously empty with a noise coming from the cupboard; submarines can communicate with each other solely through music. Sometimes, just a sideways step is necessary to enrich a commonplace. In football, the ball can be kicked out of the pitch, fly through the window of a house and land in someone's bath. Instantaneously the game of football can be forgotten and the unfortunate person in the bath becomes the focal point of the story. A seemingly important image like rice pudding can be

vitalised by being used to make a sculpture which comes alive . . . 'Joe Bloggs', the most commonplace of all characters suggested by children is, however, a non-starter. This anti-hero has a built-in negative wholeness which can kill a word journey at its inception by sheer banality. So, as with popular imagery, I try to by-pass him by saying something like, 'But in the orange tree over Joe Blogg's head came the noise of a . . . ?'

Convenience images, like convenience food, provide a quick solution to a problem, but the best food is that which is prepared with loving care, and story making needs the same attention to detail. Sometimes, when accepting a commonplace, say a milkman, I endeavour to winkle out of the class a detailed description of his appearance: 'Not only does he wear a buttercup but he wears it because . . . ? And why does he walk with a limp?'

In one story improvisation a tree was suggested as a subject. It would be hard to think of a more basic form, but the class made it into the first tree in the world. (Later at the end of the story it became the last tree in the world.)

Another door is marked **Personal Images**. Sometimes characters or situations from a story a child is reading are offered as improvisation material. On several occasions I have been unsure when I am being given a contribution from the child's imagination or a total 'lift' from a work of children's fiction. At times children sense my uncertainty and tell me its from such and such a book, or more often it materialises that the source is from the class teacher's end-of-the-day story. If some remarkable name, place or event comes with explosive spontaneity then the chances are that either you have a born writer in your midst or are being given material from a book or film. Of course, a method of stimulating children's creative writing is to give them well-known characters from fiction with the task of inventing new adventures for them. This is an excellent approach but the puritanical streak in my nature always aims for that which is wholly self-made. So when published images of the child's personal acquaintance arise in this way I try to branch off elsewhere: 'Well yes, she did come to Bluebeard's Castle, but before she got to the drawbridge what should happen but . . . ?' Worst of all images are the fairies, giants, witches and goblins which are archetypes lying just beneath the surface of the child's imagination. A lot of character surgery must happen here, for these images must be transformed if anything worthwhile is to come out of them. When witches are suggested I give a short lead at first: 'But the witch was unhappy. Why?' and then longer: 'She had a dreadful secret, what was it?' and then longer still: 'So she became a washing machine and . . .' And so once again we climb away from death by stereotype!

One important rule with story improvisation is never to reject a contribution. However stereotyped or downright boring a suggestion is I always accept, but then, by using one of the techniques described above (and in the following pages), I redirect it to something more promising. And what if one's overtures to a class meet with a resounding silence? My solution to this non-starter is to use either a real object like an umbrella or small box, or an imaginery one, to give the class something concrete on which to build ideas. (I describe some of the strategies I use to get a story off the ground in the sections in this book which deal with story making with children.)

The greatest gift a story conductor can bestow is the illusion that he or she is not really there; that the story is evolving from within the class and all one is doing is listening to what is being made. The role of the conductor is a very important one suggesting where necessary, 'standing back' when the story flows, sensing when the story is going nowhere and injecting new ideas and possibilities; 'feeling' the pressure in the room and the spirit of creativity which is carrying the story along; getting every child involved in some way, however small. Really, the conductor is making the story from the raw materials projected by the children but it must never seem that way. Only if they feel the story has been *their* creation will the experience have been a success and achieve the objective of showing each individual child that they can invent a story.

The teacher as a story performer

There is for every teacher a moment of panic when facing a class for the first time. The beginning of a worthwhile project requires all the acting skills a teacher can muster, for the child must be seduced by what is being offered. It is a combination of charm, salesmanship and the beguiling attraction of enthusiasm. But with story making there is another necessary quality and this can only be described as a ritualistic presence – of making the story a living organism growing into the aural space of the classroom.

Facing a group of children for the first time, I try to cover my nervousness and say, 'Let's make a story'. After more than twenty years of teaching I still feel the same sense of inadequacy when about to 'go on stage' with a class. At these first few words the instinctive performer inside me rises to take my place, as it were, and another, normally hidden person takes over. It never ceases to surprise and excite me when this happens, for in this state of go-between, betwixt child and the magical power of the story telling imagination, I both hold the story and present it back to the inventors as an audience. When performing this dual role of coordinator and orator I am aware at times of a rigid search on the horizon for some material substance to wrap around the skeletal form of the story. Children grow weary, tire easily and have a low threshold of boredom. Timing is therefore crucial and new ideas, characters, a shift of direction must fill the story like helium so that it can rise. At times this searching of the horizon brings only empty space. At this point everyone senses a breakdown and for a moment the force from within the imagination is eclipsed, but then (and I have never known this not to happen) there is a regeneration of ideas, small and snowflake like or as large as a dream, which picks the story up and sends it off again. Practice is essential. The ability to lift a story off the ground and, like a kite, to fly it on a tight string, comes from a regular exercising of the imagination. The class must believe in the teacher as a story teller if they are to have the confidence to make a story themselves. And this has as much to do with body language as the story itself. There are techniques of facial gesture and poise that are essential to good story improvisation. There is a certain way of lifting the eyebrows and slowing speech when one wishes to give the impression that one knows what will come next. Instinctively, nearly the whole class is bursting to get their contribution adopted in place of the story conductor. Even when a story has sunk, exaggerated gestures can bring it back to life again:

'. . . and in the field there was a . . . brick wall which she had not noticed before and when she got CLOSE TO IT WHAT SHOULD SHE FIND BUT . . .'

One then takes an exaggerated implosion of air as if about to make an important announcement while one's eyes say to the class 'Well what is it to be?' Teachers sometimes imagine that there are special gifts made available to a story director but the techniques used are very similar to those used in daily classroom management. The faked displeasure, the 'I'm waiting-for-you-John' look, the coy smile when you want a child to run an errand for you, are just a few of the vast repertoire of body language gestures that comprise the teacher's communication equipment. It only requires a readjustment for these gestures to be adapted to story telling presentations. One of the ways a teacher holds the attention of a class is by slowing normal speech speeds 'poco a poco rallentando' whilst simultaneously accenting consonants and elongating vowels with an upward crescendo:

	accent	*hold syllable slightly*
now this is	Very	Important

slower ....

mp ——————————————— *f*

This example contains almost the same intonation as a dramatic situation in story telling:

but what should she find *but*

slower ....

mp ——————————————— *f*

Every teacher is able to project his/her personality through the theatre of story making. It isn't all that different to having a conversation with someone in which you describe an experience you have had. I remember visiting a school and improvising a story with children. Afterwards the class teacher said to me 'I couldn't do that'. At break time over coffee she described an argument she'd had with the manager of a shop. She acted out the dialogue she had had with him. It was an almost professional performance. But she was *unaware* that she had the ability to communicate through her intuitive acting skills and was as much a performer as I was.

3 Children's self-made books

The moment I walked into the year five teaching area at Brookburn Primary School I knew that it was a happy place. I don't think anyone has ever been able to describe what that feeling is, but everyone who knows schools, knows what I mean. Barbara, the class teacher and deputy head, had made it that way, for her personality could be felt everywhere, from the pastel-tinted skeins of wool hanging from the ceiling, to the way the children sat at their tables.

After the usual introduction I told the class we were going to make story books and took two from the carrier bag at my feet. It was a very colourful bag, deliberately so, for it is part of my regalia as performer-teacher. To have walked into the room, books in hand would have weakened their potential as attention holders. A plain or prosaically adorned bag does not provoke anything. A plastic carrier bag of the supermarket variety is an image of disinterest. No, the bags I use are usually made by me, and so can be modelled to suit any situation which is encountered. The manner in which one removes a book from the bag, and the position in which one holds it at the moment of delivery is crucial. The bag must be held at least waist high so that everyone can see it and there must be a period of fumbling, as if searching for something. At this point I look around the room and wait until every eye is on my 'book hand', and when that has been accomplished the book is produced.

So it was on that Monday afternoon that I showed them two of my collection of illustrated story books. They were Terry Jones' *Fairy Tales* with beautifully transluscent illustrations on rough water-colour paper by Michael Foreman, and *Hans Anderson's Fairy Tales* illustrated by the inimitable Heath Robinson. These sharp, silhouetted pictures are good distance display material for a whole class. I told them how this book had been given to me by my father when I was four years old and that I could remember the moment when I opened it for the first time and fell instantly and eternally in love with the magic of illustrated books. I invited their comments and questions on both books, but only briefly, because I would return to them later, and at this point the class was eagerly awaiting the activity they sensed was on the way.

I put my hand to my top shirt pocket and asked the class to guess what was inside. Hands shot up – 'money', 'a mouse', 'a pebble', 'a pen'. As these guesses were volunteered I slowly produced from my pocket a round, highly decorated bronze object. 'Well, what is it?' I said. One child thought it was a jewellery box and another the top to a walking stick. But it was neither of these. I explained to them it was the top of a Tibetan prayer wheel brought back from Darjeeling many years earlier. I had always thought that the wheel was a sealed unit, but to my amazement only recently I was showing it to a class of children when one of them said 'Look, the top comes off'. Inside we found a scroll of paper inscribed with a Tibetan prayer. It had lain undiscovered in the wheel for over twenty years. I collect small boxes and ask for them as Christmas presents from friends. A condition I make is that something has to be inside it. Some boxes contain dried leaves, others buttons, another may hold a tiny model of a New York water hydrant. One bamboo box holds Guatemalan worry dolls and another box lined with velvet opens to reveal a marble egg.

Having something visual is always a good starter with children for it fixes their gaze and concentrates attention. I used my catch phrase 'Let's make a story' and added, 'not about this container, but a box'. I have reproduced the oral exchange which followed below. My own speech is in brackets. Children's responses are unbracketed. Where several responses were made the one which was accepted into the story is in italics.

(Who does the box belong to?) A girl. (What's her name?) Susan. (And where does

Susan live?) In a house. (Can we make our home different from ordinary homes?) It's very small. It's made of chocolate. *It has lots and lots of rooms*. (So Susan is in her house full of lots of rooms with this box. Where did it come from?) China. Woolworths. Her mum and dad gave it to her. *She found it*. It was a present. (Now this box that Susan found was rather beautiful. Can we describe it?) It was red and gold. It had lots of flowers painted on it. *It was made of something very precious*. (Now when Susan tried to take the lid off the box it wouldn't come off so what did she do?) She wished it off. *She got her father's tool box*. (Yes, and what then?) She used a tool to get it off. *She threw it against a wall and it opened*. (And inside was . . . ?) A tiny elephant. *A little girl*. A magic potion. A house. (How did this little girl get inside the box?) She was put there by a spell. *She climbed in and couldn't get out*. It was her house. (But now she was free and the first thing she wanted to do was . . . ?) Play outside. *Go shopping*. Search for a box she had lost. (So Susan went shopping. Where did she go?) To a computer shop. To Tesco's. *To a market*. (And at the market she saw?) *A lovely dress*. A pineapple. (And she wanted it so much but she didn't have any money so she . . . ?) Asked the man if she could have it. (And he said 'No, but . . .') 'You can have it if you say a spell that will give me lots of money'. (So the little girl said the name of her favourite food very quickly and that cast a spell. But it didn't bring the man money. What did it do instead?) It made his stall fall

down. *It made the dress disappear*. (So the little girl and Susan ran and ran until . . . ?) They reached a supermarket. *They got home*. (Now who can bring the story to a close?) The girl climbed back into the box and fell asleep. *She turned into a tree*. They both hid inside a cupboard. (Can we give the story a more exciting ending. Remember the box . . .) The tree had hundreds of little boxes growing off it.

This improvisation had flowed quite easily. Ideas were forthcoming with little prompting from me. We were now ready to begin the main activity part of the lesson – writing the story. With a class I know, I would present a wholly new stimulus at this point to avoid a repetition of the story just told. But I knew nothing of these children and as there were thirty in the class I left them with a story on which they could fall back if and when their own ideas waned.

There was a lively atmosphere in the room, so I used as few words as possible in getting them started in their rough books. I just told them to begin again with the box idea and write down whatever came to them. Some were half way down the page in minutes whilst others tapped their pencils nervously on the tables and rocked back and forth on their chairs. I spent the next hour with individuals, helping the story on its way with plot here, spelling there, worming descriptions and continuity out of others, and trying to get the first line out of one child in particular.

Concertina books

As stories became completed and corrected it was time to attend to the design of the story in book form. I showed the class a blank concertina book. I had selected this form as it is by far the easiest book to make, requiring no glueing or stitching. I had cut strips of heavy cartridge paper, folded them into five pages and cut a window out of the first page so that it could be folded forward and incorporated into the design on page two. (The window was optional and I had several book forms available without them.) The children had the option of either writing out their stories 'in best' on lined paper, or for the more adventurous, transferring the written work directly into the book.

Both approaches required the mathematical abstraction of transfer, visualising the story from exercise books to a sequence of pages. We looked again at the two illustrated books placing particular emphasis on layout and relationship of illustration to text. The children had to select the main episodes into which their story fell and transpose them to the folds of the book on which they were about to embark. We looked at examples of writer and illustrator juxtaposing their two arts. The children had to choose parts of the story suitable for visual representation; to take a place or situation from the story and realise it as a drawing so that anyone reading their story would 'see' it more clearly through the

Blackboard roughs suggesting ways of arranging words and images

Andrea's four-fold concertina book with card 'cover'

information conveyed in the illustrations. The concertina books were given out so that the visualising transfer could be as concrete as possible – they needed to see the book in front of them. I drew some block shapes on the board showing how words and pictures can be arranged together in patterns.

I was to find that the children had an inner sense of design referred to earlier, and that apart from one or two cases visual images and blocks of words fell into a natural order. The need to fit their story into a ready-made virgin book with fixed number of pages was a new and demanding challenge. Some children who found writing a struggle would space out blocks of writing so thinly that large areas became territories for illustrative work. Conversely, stories which developed through a series of episodes needed the area covered by both sides of the concertina folds.

In comparing written work in their exercise books to that of their self-made books, the difference which struck me most was the length of written passages. For several children the story was the largest piece of writing they had accomplished. The book framework had really proved to be a stretcher of the imagination which, in turn, projected skills required to make written language work for children. As one teacher who came to see year five's books said, 'Making a book really does push the words along'.

Concertina book

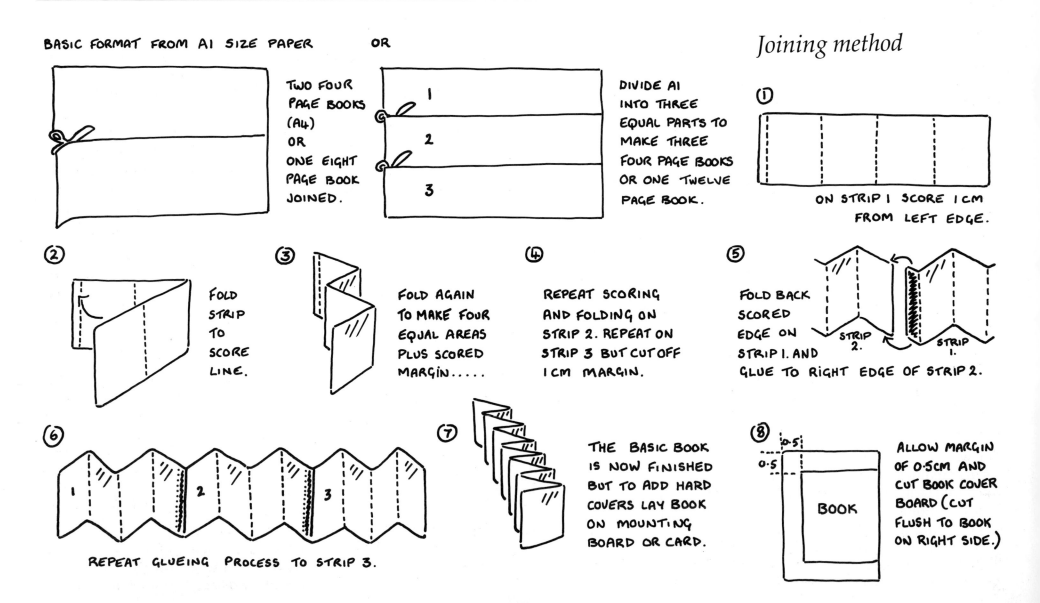

BASIC FORMAT FROM A1 SIZE PAPER   OR

Joining method

TWO FOUR PAGE BOOKS (A4) OR ONE EIGHT PAGE BOOK JOINED.

1
2
3

DIVIDE A1 INTO THREE EQUAL PARTS TO MAKE THREE FOUR PAGE BOOKS OR ONE TWELVE PAGE BOOK.

① ON STRIP 1 SCORE 1CM FROM LEFT EDGE.

② FOLD STRIP TO SCORE LINE.

③ FOLD AGAIN TO MAKE FOUR EQUAL AREAS PLUS SCORED MARGIN.....

④ REPEAT SCORING AND FOLDING ON STRIP 2. REPEAT ON STRIP 3 BUT CUT OFF 1CM MARGIN.

⑤ FOLD BACK SCORED EDGE ON STRIP 1. AND GLUE TO RIGHT EDGE OF STRIP 2.

STRIP 2.   STRIP 1.

⑥ 1   2   3

REPEAT GLUEING PROCESS TO STRIP 3.

⑦ THE BASIC BOOK IS NOW FINISHED BUT TO ADD HARD COVERS LAY BOOK ON MOUNTING BOARD OR CARD.

⑧ 0.5 0.5

BOOK

ALLOW MARGIN OF 0.5CM AND CUT BOOK COVER BOARD (CUT FLUSH TO BOOK ON RIGHT SIDE.)

(9) DUPLICATE FOR BACK COVER (IF THIN BOARD IS USED MAKE FOUR COVERS AND GLUE TOGETHER).

(10) TO MAKE BOOK SPINE CUT A STRIP OF CARD THE SAME HEIGHT AS THE COVER BOARDS AND 4CM WIDE. (REDUCE THICKNESS FOR BOOKS OF LESS THAN 12 PAGES.)

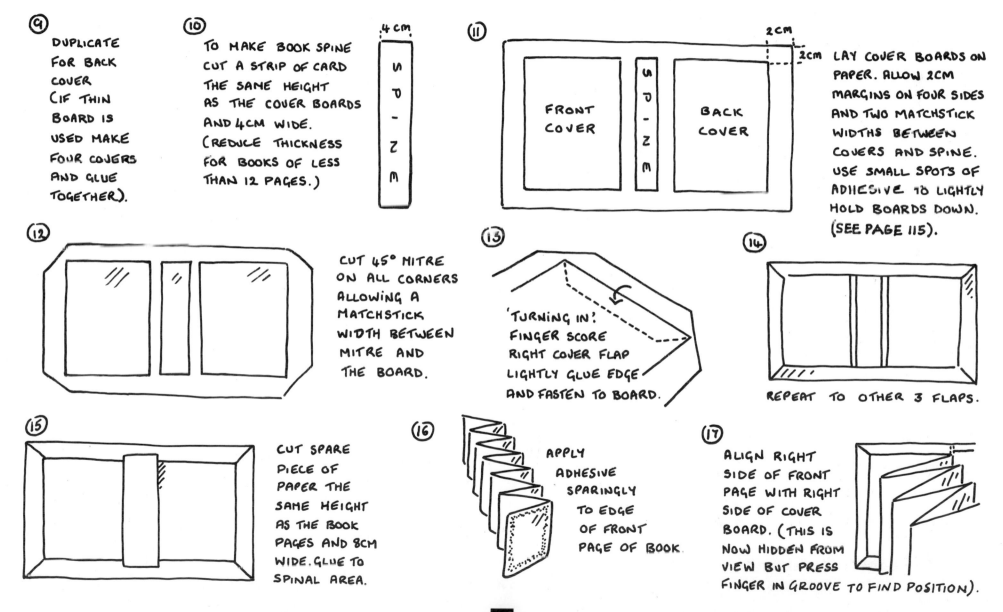

.4 CM

SPINE

(11) FRONT COVER   SPINE   BACK COVER

2CM
2CM

LAY COVER BOARDS ON PAPER. ALLOW 2CM MARGINS ON FOUR SIDES AND TWO MATCHSTICK WIDTHS BETWEEN COVERS AND SPINE. USE SMALL SPOTS OF ADHESIVE TO LIGHTLY HOLD BOARDS DOWN. (SEE PAGE 115).

(12)

CUT 45° MITRE ON ALL CORNERS ALLOWING A MATCHSTICK WIDTH BETWEEN MITRE AND THE BOARD.

(13) 'TURNING IN'. FINGER SCORE RIGHT COVER FLAP LIGHTLY GLUE EDGE AND FASTEN TO BOARD.

(14)

REPEAT TO OTHER 3 FLAPS.

(15)

CUT SPARE PIECE OF PAPER THE SAME HEIGHT AS THE BOOK PAGES AND 8CM WIDE. GLUE TO SPINAL AREA.

(16) APPLY ADHESIVE SPARINGLY TO EDGE OF FRONT PAGE OF BOOK.

(17) ALIGN RIGHT SIDE OF FRONT PAGE WITH RIGHT SIDE OF COVER BOARD. (THIS IS NOW HIDDEN FROM VIEW BUT PRESS FINGER IN GROOVE TO FIND POSITION).

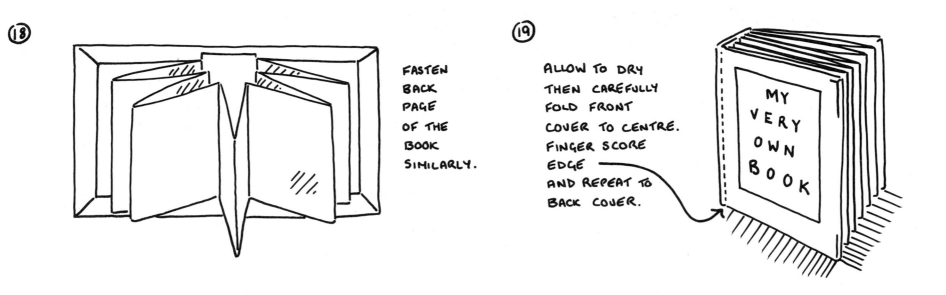

⑱ FASTEN BACK PAGE OF THE BOOK SIMILARLY.

⑲ ALLOW TO DRY THEN CAREFULLY FOLD FRONT COVER TO CENTRE. FINGER SCORE EDGE AND REPEAT TO BACK COVER.

MY VERY OWN BOOK

Open spine binding

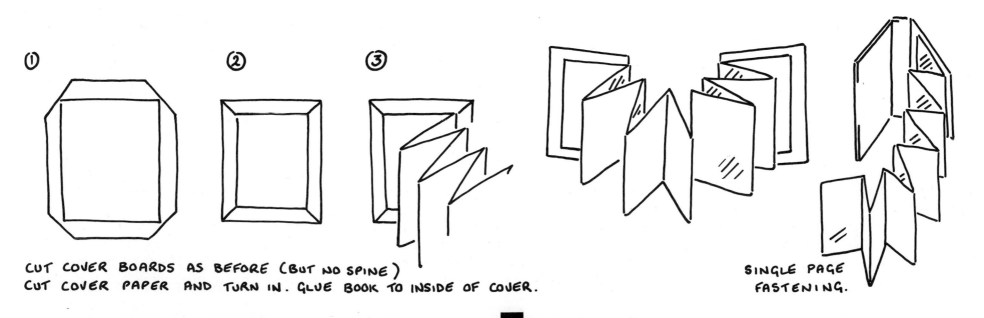

① ② ③

CUT COVER BOARDS AS BEFORE (BUT NO SPINE)
CUT COVER PAPER AND TURN IN. GLUE BOOK TO INSIDE OF COVER.

SINGLE PAGE FASTENING.

4 *Learning through book forming*

In my very first book project with children (page 20) they made concertina books because the stories they were making suggested the basic, continuous, unstitched method. Nearly always the story came first and the book developed from that. As my experience of working with children grew, unconventional ways of making books happened as a natural progression of the activity. It was 'playing' with paper, cutting and folding origami style, that book forms presented themselves almost, as it were, without me being aware of it. From these experiments developed the notion of a ready-made book as a stimulus for writing. Of course, a purchased exercise book is a 'ready-made' book, but these books were special because of the often intricate nature of their construction or the unusual shapes they made as 2D/3D objects. One of the rules I gave myself was that in book improvisations, nothing could be added or taken away from the basic A2/3 sheet of paper. There was something complete and holistic about this discipline as if one was obeying some kind of natural law of invention. The profusion of page pull-outs, 'pop-ups', doors and windows that presented themselves, like origami itself, needed no further justification. But the inquisitive mind would not settle at that, for each page seemed to want to tell a story. Or to put it another way, a story

wanted to tell the book. The first time I tried out the idea of a complete, ready-made book as a stimulus was with year five pupils. I chose *Book with pop-up*. This comprises ten pages, plus front and back covers with a pop-up middle section. Just as a piece of stone holds a sculpture, so this book held a story. It will be useful if at this point the reader turns to page 58 and experiences the book in question – even makes one, and then sees how Philip has so creatively visualised the story in writing, illustration and design.

Books made from one single sheet of paper demand that all visible pages contain graphic markings of some kind. Beryl, an infant teacher (see page 70) is only too aware of the frightening imposition the effect of a whole book of blank paper can have on a child when asked to 'write a story'. But these books comprise relatively few pages and as many of them are unusual in some way, there is enough visual stimulus to hold the child's interest.

I conceived these books as journeys. And just as journeys take us through doors, down roads, through events or situations, up stairs, across rivers, up into the air or on the sea, so it was that each page symbolised some episode – a story in the process of becoming. The teaching technique I adopted was to play games with these books before they were

'individualised' by children: to improvise characters and 'talk through' impromptu journeys page by page. The story shape was visualised on the blank pages: a beginning on page one, a climax at page 5 and a resolution, ending on page 10. Sometimes a door or window would 'help the story along' and move us on to a new level of story invention. Some books (like the extended concertina book, page 48 and the tall book, page 54) had a pull-out middle section so that an elongated area dictated an object of unusual proportions. This necessitated the story beginning in the middle, working backwards to page one and then taking up from the middle again and progressing to the end. This calls for a wholly different way of conceiving story writing, a technique not unknown to crime writers, who start by inventing a murdered person and then work backwards through the suspects to the killer. I'm reminded of the much-quoted statement of Marcel Duchamp 'Everything has a beginning, a middle and an end, but not necessarily in that order'. It is good for children to have their imaginations stretched in this way, and although this could be a daunting abstraction for children of average, or less than average, ability, I have never found it so. The empty book is always in front of them as they plan, explore and draft. If the story starts in the middle of the book, they can 'see' the pages moving to left and right. Mental images become implanted in these empty spaces, the stage by stage progression is of physical substance. The story writer constructs the story to match the pages (and sometimes a set number of words to the page), corresponding illustration pages prepare areas for visual representation. This structured framework liberates the imagination rather than restricts it, as might be supposed, because the child is at liberty to invent whatever he chooses and to use the book form to develop it. With numbered draft pages in front of them corresponding to the pages of the book, children can't say 'I've finished the story' when they've only reached page three and have another seven pages to go. I have been intrigued by the way children have been stimulated to write far in excess of their normal story lengths by this method. And neither is it an imposition, for the joy of making a book is a driving force to creativity. Mary said to me 'I can't wait to write about the man climbing through the bathroom window so that I can turn the page and write about him falling into the bath'. So there are two kinds of motivation going on here: (*i*) the excitement of making a book, and (*ii*) the stimulation of the pristine book itself.

The twenty-three projects from single sheets of paper which follow demonstrate different kinds of verbal and visual activities triggered by the book form. I hope they will speak for themselves, not only as learning tools for children acquiring the most basic and fundamental of writing skills, but as innovative ways of enthusing children with new challenges in communicating ideas.

Books from one sheet of paper

It is open to debate at what stage a folded card becomes a leaflet, a leaflet a booklet, a booklet a book. If necessity breeds invention then the purpose to which communication material is aimed determines the nature of the communication format. A few words with accompanying artwork fit neatly into the single fold of the greeting card. A synopsis advertising a book requires a larger area like a triple-folded A4 presentation. What is interesting to observe is the way that designers arrange the verbal/graphical/art material given to them into the constraints of the various paper sizes, folded divisions available. The children's book projects here illustrate not only how they use the book-page arrangement to stimulate creative invention but, as with professional layout artists, how they use it as a framwork in which to make a balanced harmony of words and images.

These twenty-three strategies of folded paper arrangements comprising book forming take the single fold as the point at which a book form can take shape. Without a fold we have a poster or wall display of some kind. From basic single, double, treble folds the four-folded page marks the point at which the concertina book is born. From here endless possibilities of book design make themselves available to the imaginative creator. But what is special about them is that, with the exception of applied covers in some cases, they are all produced from a single sheet of paper. Moreover, the overall sheet of paper remains intact. This has a number of advantages: (*i*) the limitations of a single sheet widens rather than restricts the range of design possibilities, as the illustrations will show; (*ii*) there is no wastage whatsoever; (*iii*) it is impossible for pages to be lost; (*iv*) cutting multiple book forms and assembly is relatively simple.

Some of the later books involve pop-up and 3D means of construction which, theoretically, place them outside the scope of this, a 2D, book. However, I have included them here because they have evolved from, and are indigenous to, the single-sheet book principal. The permutations presented are only a stimulus to the reader. Children come up to me regularly when I am engaged on a school-based project and say 'Look at this book I've invented'. Always adapt to your own need and try to avoid reproducing a ready-made scheme.

Folded cards/leaflet forms

(SEE FOLDING INSTRUCTIONS ON PAGE 68)

Folded A4 to A5 is the most basic form of all, but if thin cartridge (or duplicating paper) is used, the standing presentation will eventually tend to collapse.

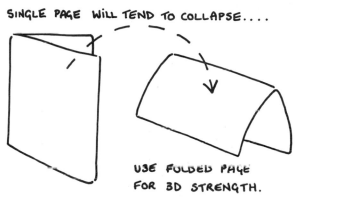

SINGLE PAGE WILL TEND TO COLLAPSE....

USE FOLDED PAGE FOR 3D STRENGTH.

PLEASE OPEN

① Folded page card

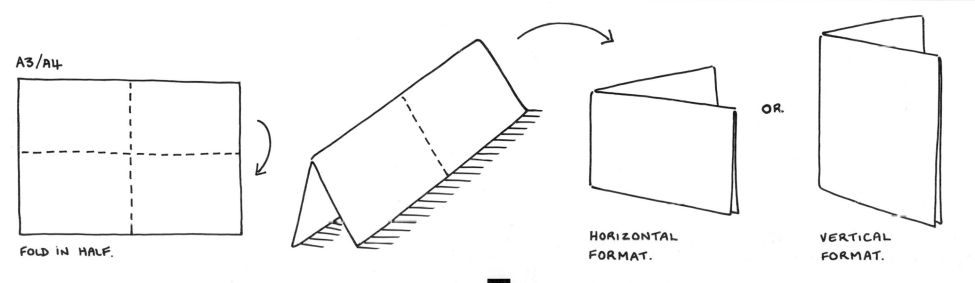

A3/A4

FOLD IN HALF.

OR.

HORIZONTAL FORMAT.

VERTICAL FORMAT.

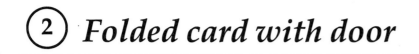

An added advantage to the double page is that doors and windows can be cut to provide stimulus for thematic story development. *The Music Soldier* by Daniel (5) shows this to good effect, as does the same strategy in developed form, *The Castle House* by Jennifer (6).

'The Music Soldier' by Daniel (5)

'The Castle House' by Jennifer (6) Door closed . . . Door open . . .

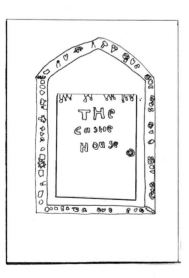

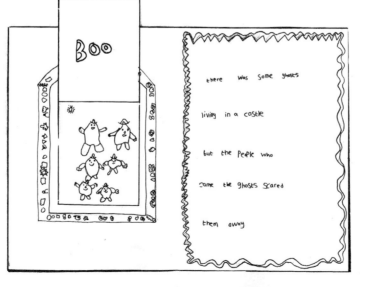

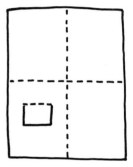

OPEN FLAP TO REVEAL ARTWORK BENEATH.

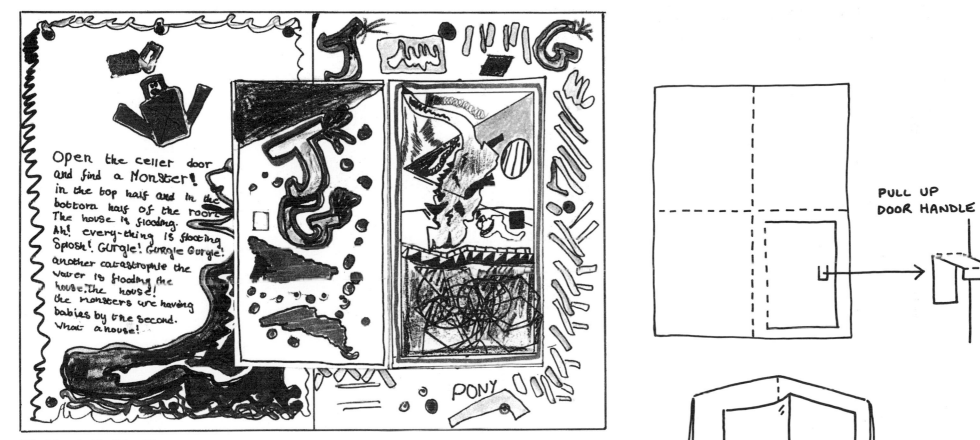

'The Monster' by John (8)

PULL UP
DOOR HANDLE

The Monster by John (8) intensifies the door theme by cutting a pull-up door handle. The quality of John's artwork has been stimulated by the novelty of the folded presentation.

Here two 'doors' of equal proportion enclose a back panel with vaulted roof.

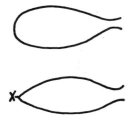

① A4 HORIZONTAL

FOLD OUTER EDGES TO CENTRE. TO FIND CENTRE WITHOUT CREASING PAPER MAKE A LOOP. MARK HALFWAY POINT ALONG TOP EDGE WITH FINGERNAIL 'X'.

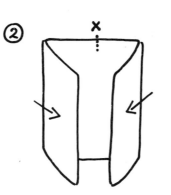

②

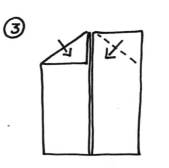

③

FOLD CORNERS TO CENTRE

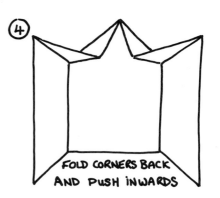

④

FOLD CORNERS BACK AND PUSH INWARDS

When laid top-down, Kate (8) thought that the form looked like a frog. This stimulated frog artwork on the outside central panel, and a story 'The Ferocious Frog' on the outside (door) panels.

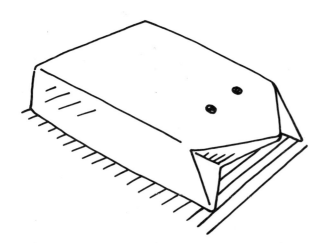

'The Ferocious Frog' by Kate (8)

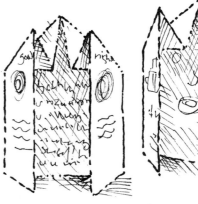

④ Presentation card

A variation of the tabernacle told is to cut the paper as shown to make an unusual tuck-in fold-over.

①

A4

FOLD ON HORIZONTAL.

②

MAKE LOOP OF STRIP, ENSURING THAT FOLDS ARE AVOIDED.

③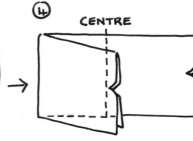

CUT "V" SLOT THROUGH THE FOUR SHEETS.

④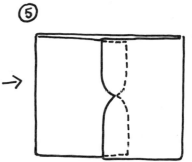

CENTRE

ON HORIZONTAL PLANE FOLD LEFT AND RIGHT FLAPS TO 1 CM BEYOND CENTRE POINT.

⑤

⑥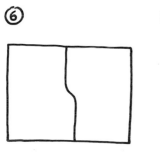

FINALLY TUCK IN BOTH FLAPS.

⑦

FINISHED FOLDER FROM VERTICAL A4 FORMAT.

VARIATIONS :-

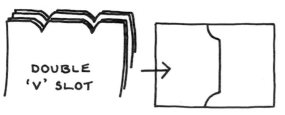

DOUBLE 'V' SLOT

This design stimulates a single folded story which is hidden and therefore thematically secret, private or in Andrew's case, ghostly. To augment the mood of ghostliness everything is back to front; the booklet opens from right to left and all the writing inside is from right to left too!

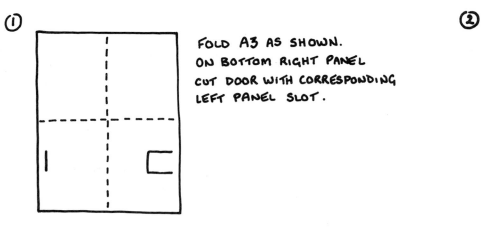

① FOLD A3 AS SHOWN. ON BOTTOM RIGHT PANEL CUT DOOR WITH CORRESPONDING LEFT PANEL SLOT.

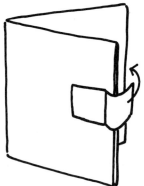

② FOLD TO A5. FOLD DOOR FLAP AROUND ....

③ AND LOCK INTO SLOT ON REVERSE.

'Ghost Hunter Secret File' by Andrew (8)

⑥ Window card

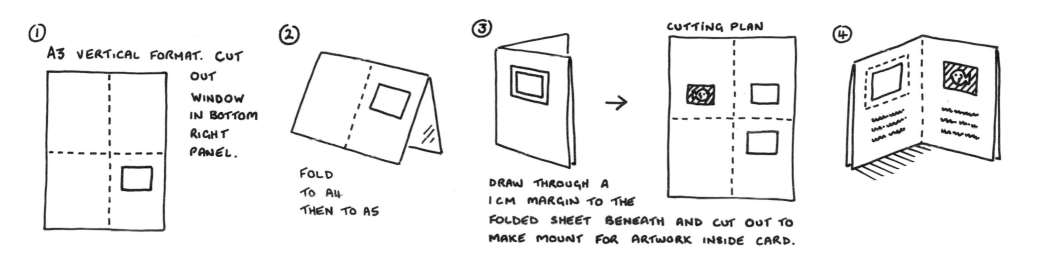

① A3 VERTICAL FORMAT. CUT OUT WINDOW IN BOTTOM RIGHT PANEL.

② FOLD TO A4 THEN TO A5

③ DRAW THROUGH A 1CM MARGIN TO THE FOLDED SHEET BENEATH AND CUT OUT TO MAKE MOUNT FOR ARTWORK INSIDE CARD.

CUTTING PLAN

④

This method of presentation produces a double mounted piece of artwork supported by writing. Moira (9) made a white line on coloured background illustration of a small trinket box in the shape of a duck. This was made by inscribing the design with a hard pencil (HB,1H) through tracing paper to cartridge beneath. This makes a light incision in the cartridge which can be crayoned over to produce the unique white line effect shown. The finished artwork was glued into the picture area, the story written to accompany it and a title incorporated into the cover design. Finally, a decorative border was applied to the mounted area.

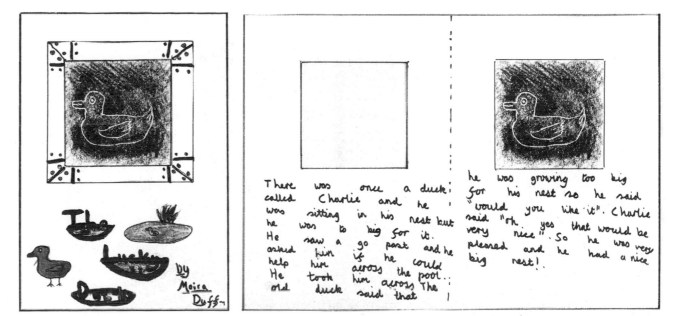

Cover

Inside card

⑦ Haiku poem fold and origami envelope

Before moving on to the next stage of basic books, I want to include a very intimate interrelationship of two sheets of A4 paper. The simplicity of beauty is so inspiringly manifested in the Haiku poem (lines of 5,7,5 syllables) and what could be more appropriate than a simple origami envelope to hold the words?

John (9) wrote:

'When the day is gone
The moon and stars shine brightly
And dreams fill the world.'

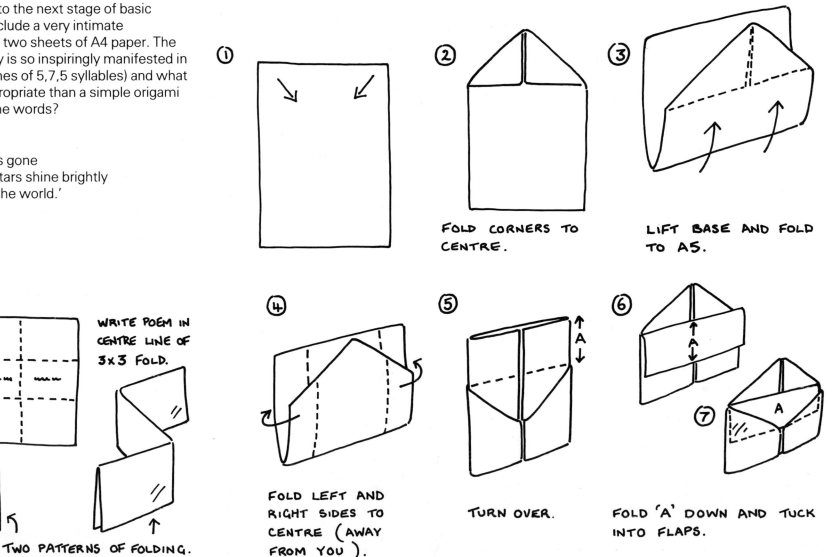

①

② FOLD CORNERS TO CENTRE.

③ LIFT BASE AND FOLD TO A5.

WRITE POEM IN CENTRE LINE OF 3x3 FOLD.

TWO PATTERNS OF FOLDING.

④ FOLD LEFT AND RIGHT SIDES TO CENTRE (AWAY FROM YOU).

⑤ TURN OVER.

⑥ ⑦ FOLD 'A' DOWN AND TUCK INTO FLAPS.

Moving away from cards and leaflet-type formats, the four-fold concertina represents the most basic of non-cutting books. Because of its adaptability, it finds itself in several forms in this book, but here it is shown in its simplest version.

'My Holiday at the Lakes, by Lee (7) illustrates the basic concertina book in an A4 (reduced from A3) version.

'My Holiday at the Lakes' by Lee (7)

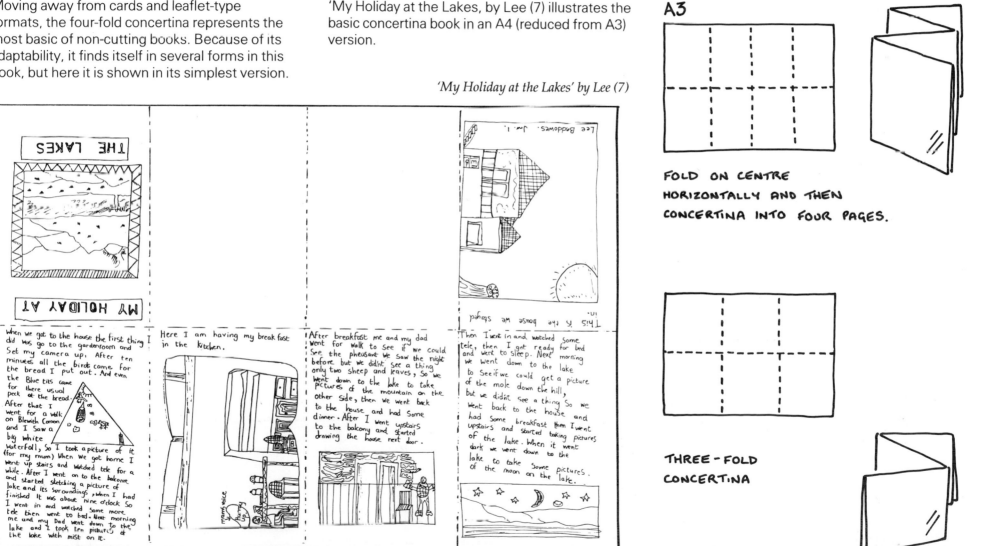

A3

FOLD ON CENTRE HORIZONTALLY AND THEN CONCERTINA INTO FOUR PAGES.

THREE-FOLD CONCERTINA

⑨ *Irregular concertina book*

Sarah (8) invented this one – 'The Magic Tree Seed' – a series of concertina folds which increase in size. Her story, about a growing tree, prompted the book's invention, so that 'the book could grow like a tree'.

'The Magic Tree Seed' by Sarah (8)

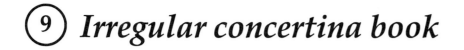

A4

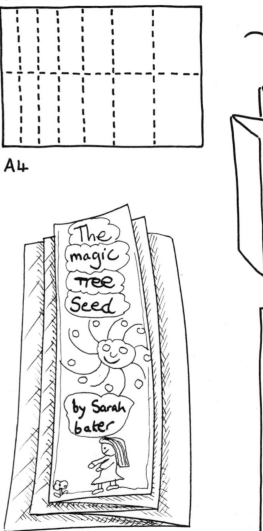

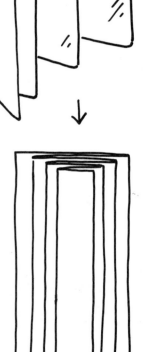

⑩ *Origami book*

The simplicity of this book makes it immediately accessible for large-class production whilst being more novel than a simple folded concertina. If children are capable of using scissors, they can make the whole book themselves. I must have seen several hundred origami books by children, on every conceivable theme from stories to recipes, local studies to illustrated journals. I have illustrated two contrasting styles.

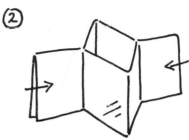

① A3/A4 FOLD TO EIGHT. CUT THROUGH CENTRE SECTIONS. FOLD ON HORIZONTAL.

② PUSH LEFT AND RIGHT ENDS TO CENTRE.

③ FOLD ROUND TO FORM BOOK. SIX WRITING/ ARTWORK PAGES, FRONT AND BACK COVERS.

'My Best Friend' by Lisa (6)

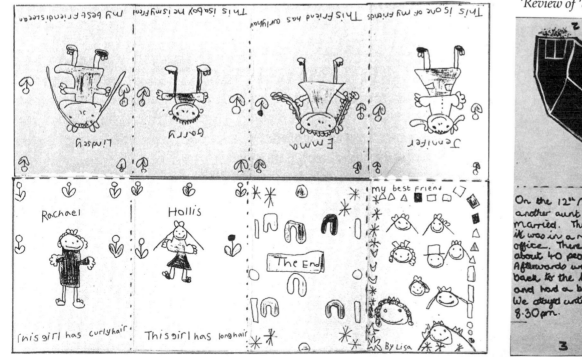

'Review of '88' by Rosalind (10)

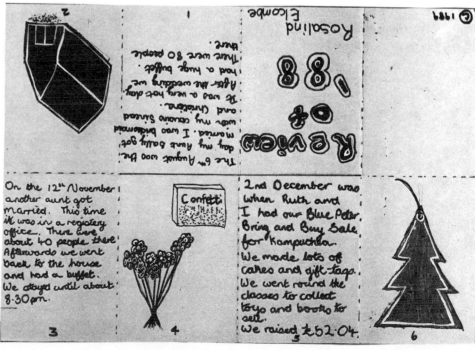

There are many ways of arranging the origami form into an environmental book. One example is by David (9) and his 'Madhouse'. The pushed-out middle section is realised as the room of a house flanked by house entrance panels. Doors and windows have been cut into the three-dimensional book with some panels reserved for the story. This was organised as follows: a frightening account of spooky goings-on on Halloween night – developed from the stage by stage assembly of the Madhouse artwork.

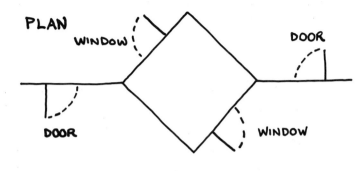

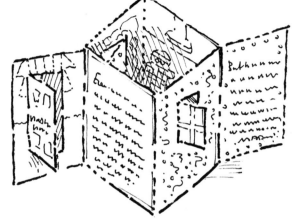

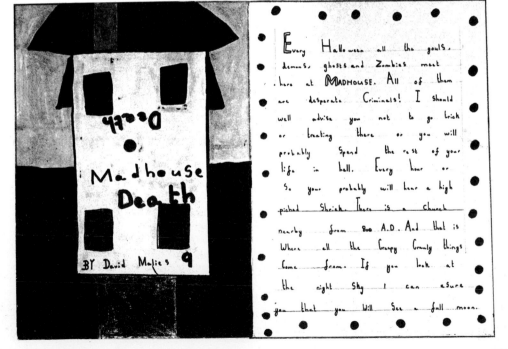

'Madhouse' by David (9)

Every Halloween all the goul's, demons, ghosts and Zombies meet here at MADHOUSE. All of them are desperate Criminals! I should well advise you not to go trick or treating there or you will probably Spend the rest of your life in hell. Every hour or So your probably will hear a high pitched Shriek. There is a Church nearby from 800 A.D. And that is Where all the Creepy Crawly things Come from. If you look at the night Sky I can assure you that you Will See a full moon.

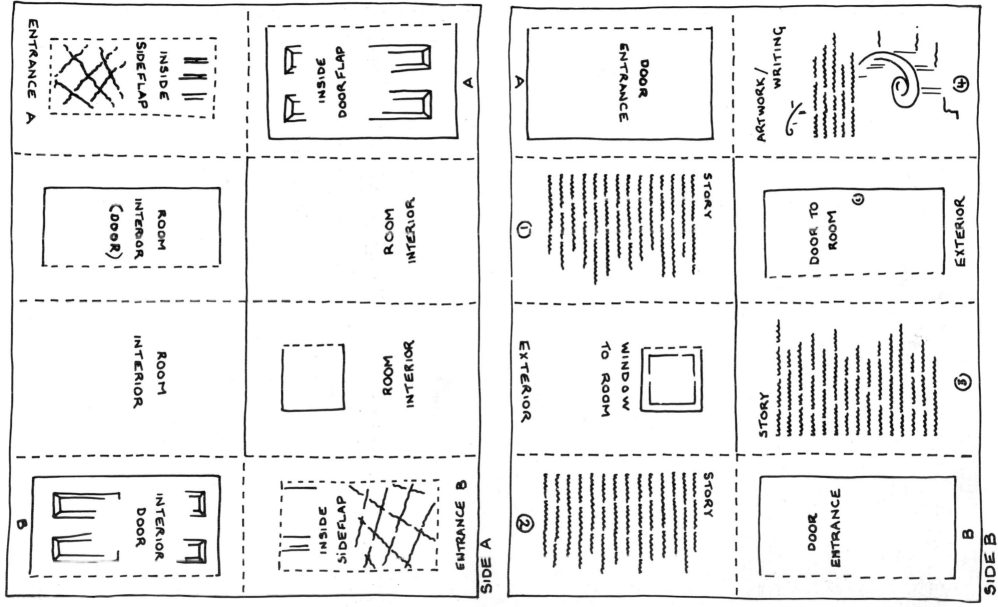

SIDE A

ENTRANCE A

INSIDE SIDEFLAP

A — INSIDE DOOR FLAP

ROOM INTERIOR (DOOR)

ROOM INTERIOR

ROOM INTERIOR

ROOM INTERIOR

B — INTERIOR DOOR

INSIDE SIDEFLAP

ENTRANCE B

SIDE B

A — DOOR ENTRANCE

④ ARTWORK / WRITING

① STORY

⑤ DOOR TO ROOM — EXTERIOR

EXTERIOR — WINDOW TO ROOM

③ STORY

② STORY

B — DOOR ENTRANCE

Story and pictures in 3 triangular sequences . . .

One of the conventions of basic, one-sheet books is that the pages tend to be of the A5 format. A way of arriving at a different shape book from an A2 base is as follows:

① FOLD CORNER TO EDGE AND REPEAT FROM TOP CORNER TO FORM DIAGONAL CROSS.

② MAKE VERTICAL CREASES AT 'A' AND HORIZONTAL CREASE AT 'B'. CUT AS SHOWN.

③ FOLD TRIANGLE 'X' 'UNDER OVER' UNTIL FORM IS COMPLETED.

④ TURN TO HORIZONTAL POSITION. OPEN BOOK PAGES AND FOLD IN CORNERS BEHIND TRIANGULAR PAGES.

⑤ COMPLETED BOOK.

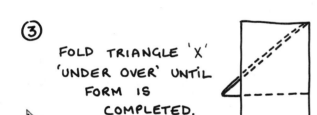

Front cover

'The Flower Lady' by Jennie (9)

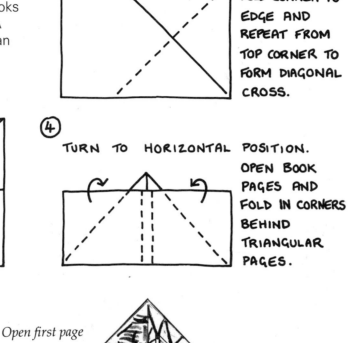

Open first page

Once there was a flower person and she loved sweets! But she could never get any.

This is another book which was stimulated by experimental illustrations. The technique is to cut forms – tree, house, figure – from fairly thick cartridge and then make a 'frottage' rubbing with wax crayons through thinner paper placed on top. The surface quality this gives is quite different to any other technique and lends itself well to book illustration (see page 35). Jennie's cut-outs for 'The Flower Lady' were a flower, sweet, and a cat, and these illustrations evoke a fantasy world which inspired an imaginative, dreamy environment in which her story could take shape.

⑬ *Fantasy window concertina book*

One of the most popular single sheet books with children is described next. A conventional four-fold concertina book is made from horizontally folded A2, but instead of leaving the pages blank, hinged openings are cut into the four folds. This approach has already been discussed, but here I show a more developed way of working.

A2

HINGED OPENINGS GIVEN
TO THE CLASS AS A SOURCE
OF STORY STIMULATION.

'Blast Off' by Matthew and Davydd (10) (openings closed)

Shut the air-lock door.
Get ready for blast-off.
5, 4, 3, 2, 1.
Blast off.

Here is moon beam
Freadie, the astronaut
See what he looks like
Smile back!

Landing on the moon,
we see a castle.
Argh, we see an alien
Let's run!

In the space ship.
Ready for blast-off
5, 4, 3, 2, 1.
We are now in space.
Look at Earth.

Experiment by cutting folded doors, windows and openings into the bottom panels as shown. An added challenge is to cut shapes in a free, unpreconceived way. The task is then to give meaning to them in story form. This form of presentation is exemplified by two groups using the same shaped openings. What is fascinating is the contrasting imagery derived from them (see next page). The dedication to design, layout, handwriting and story illustrates just how powerful an incentive an imaginatively prepared challenge is to children.

Cover design

Openings open

Shut the air-lock door. Get ready for blast-off. 5, 4, 3, 2, 1. Blast off

Here is moon beam Freadie, the astronaut. See what he looks like. Smile back!

Landing on the moon, we see a castle. Argh we see an alien. Let's run!

Phew! we escaped

In the space ship. Ready for blast-off 5, 4, 3, 2, 1. We are now in space. Look at Earth.

'The Teddy Bears Picnic'
by Karen and Lisa (10)

Doors closed

Doors open

(14) *Superimposed door book*

The opening 'door and window'-style book can be engineered as a single page presentation. I am indebted to Janet, one of my BEd students, for this invention.

Although the prospect of cutting so many apertures is a daunting proposition, using the multiple cutting technique quickens the process of manufacture for a whole class. A simpler approach would be to reduce the number of openings.

This is possibly the most complex of the books suggested here, although the cutting and folding procedure is really quite simple. In Matthew's book, he traces a journey into Dracula's wardrobe to the glass where he keeps his false teeth!

FOLD A2 TO A5s

DRAW DOOR ON FRONT OF BOOK, OPEN OUT AND CUT.
FOLD DOWN AGAIN TO A5. OPEN DOOR AND DRAW
THROUGH NO 2 DOOR.
REPEAT PROCESS TO DOOR NO 7.

①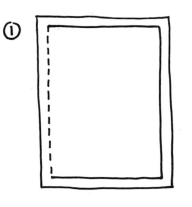

②

③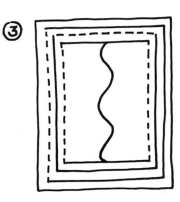

④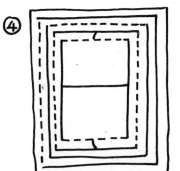

⑤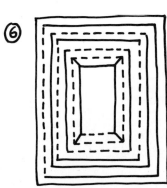

⑥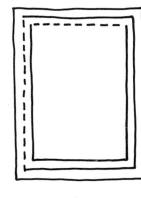

⑦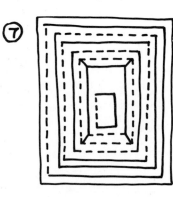

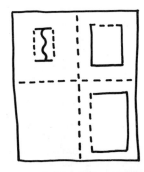

SIMPLIFIED A3 VERSION
USING 3 DOORS.

➡

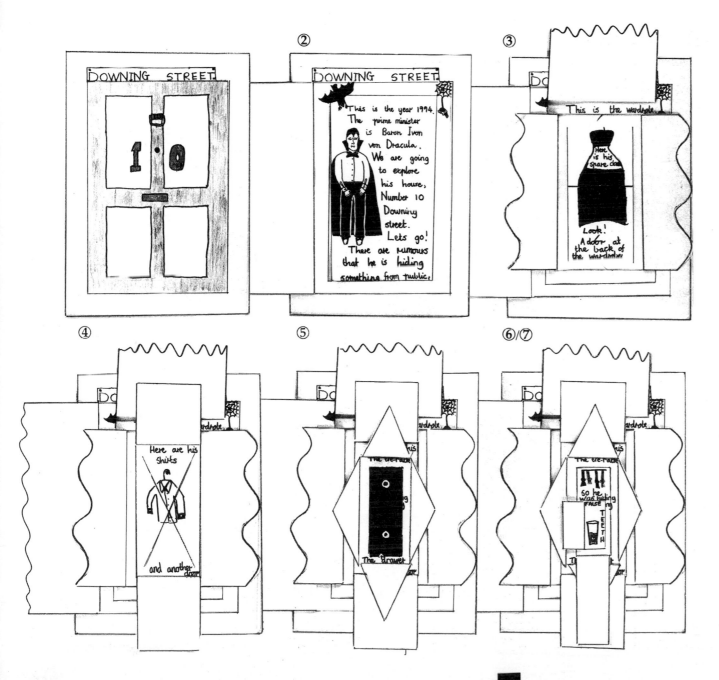

② DOWNING STREET

This is the year 1994. The prime minister is Baron Ivon von Dracula. We are going to explore his house, Number 10 Downing street. Lets go! There are rumours that he is hiding something from public.

③ This is the wardrobe

Here is his spare cloak

Look! A door at the back of the wardrobe

④ Here are his Shirts

and another door

⑤ The wardrobe

The drawer

⑥/⑦ The wardrobe

So he was hiding false TEETH

'Downing Street' by Matthew (10)

47

⑮ *Extended concertina book 3 × 6*

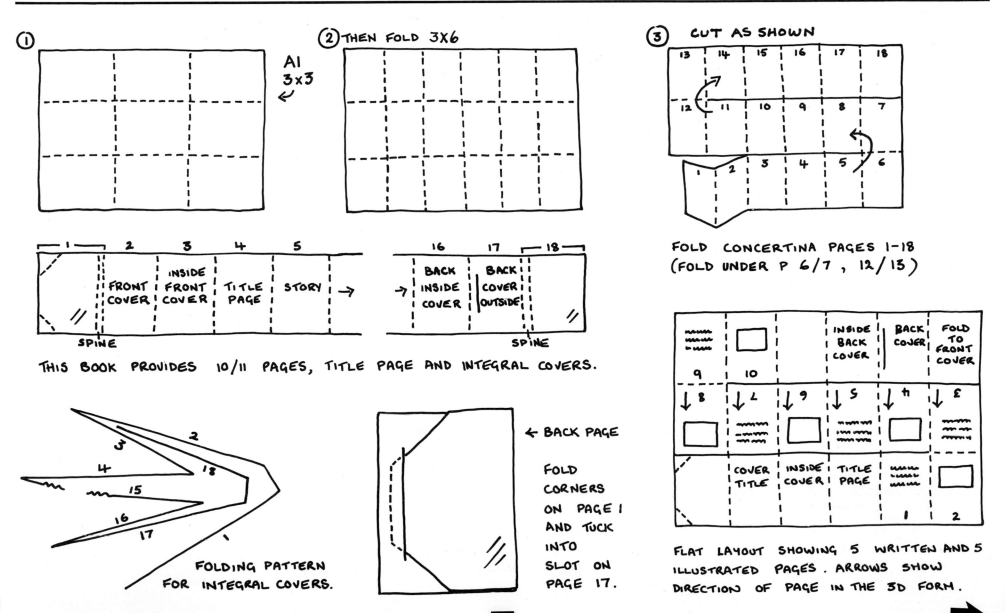

①

A1 3×3 ←

② THEN FOLD 3×6

③ CUT AS SHOWN

13	14	15	16	17	18
12	11	10	9	8	7
1	2	3	4	5	6

FOLD CONCERTINA PAGES 1-18
(FOLD UNDER P 6/7 , 12/13)

	1	2	3	4	5
SPINE	FRONT COVER	INSIDE FRONT COVER	TITLE PAGE	STORY	→

	16	17	18
→	BACK INSIDE COVER	BACK COVER OUTSIDE	SPINE

THIS BOOK PROVIDES 10/11 PAGES, TITLE PAGE AND INTEGRAL COVERS.

FOLDING PATTERN FOR INTEGRAL COVERS.

← BACK PAGE

FOLD CORNERS ON PAGE 1 AND TUCK INTO SLOT ON PAGE 17.

9	10		INSIDE BACK COVER	BACK COVER	FOLD TO FRONT COVER
↓8	↓7	↓6	↓5	↓4	↓3
	COVER TITLE	INSIDE COVER	TITLE PAGE		
				1	2

FLAT LAYOUT SHOWING 5 WRITTEN AND 5 ILLUSTRATED PAGES. ARROWS SHOW DIRECTION OF PAGE IN THE 3D FORM.

This arrangement of three A5 pages to front and back strengthens the cover. The beauty of this book is that the whole book, including covers, is produced as part of the integral folding of the A1 sheet.

'The Change of the Old Lady' – Clare (10) thought of a character and then placed five sheets of rough paper in front of her to represent the stages of the book's development:

Page 1 – An old lady called Mrs Bennett buys sweets in a sweetshop but then her top half turns into a giant pencil.

Page 2 – The shopkeeper runs out of the shop frightened, but then the bottom half of Mrs Bennett turns into a window.

Page 3 – The shopkeeper returns and is about to give Mrs Bennett her sweets when the whole of her turns into a blackboard.

Page 4 – The shopkeeper is angry with all these transformations, but Mrs Bennett suggests that it is he who is seeing things and not her changing.

Page 5 – Eventually Mrs Bennett resumes her natural self and gets her sweets.

This evidences a strategy for compiling a story to fit a ready-made book. It was prepared in stages: (*i*) selecting subject and thematic environment; (*ii*) spacing out development to set number of changes related to (*iii*) story 'shape':

Statement (page 1)
Development (pages 2,3)
'Twist' (page 4)
Resolution (page 5)

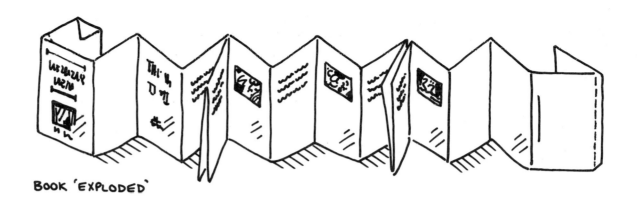

BOOK 'EXPLODED'

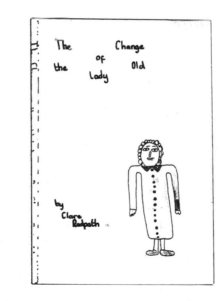

'The change of the old lady' by Clare (10)

The completed drafting exercise led to the 'writing in' of the story, followed by illustrations. Finally, title page and cover design completed the book.

This method is similar to the previous book (on page 48) except fewer pages are folded from the base sheet. I gave this book to Louise (11) and asked her to make a story to fit it. Originally it was decided that the cover would be included, integrally, but later a separate cover was added. This accounts for the book having two title pages!

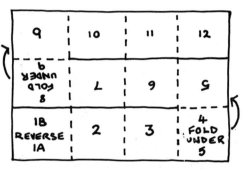

A2

FOLD AS BEFORE. DESIGNATE
PAGES AS DIAGRAM. NOTE FOLD 1 IS
USED ON BOTH SIDES HENCE 1A/B

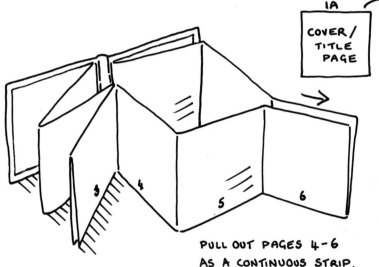

PULL OUT PAGES 4-6
AS A CONTINUOUS STRIP.

FOLD NUMBERS AT TOP OF PAGES.

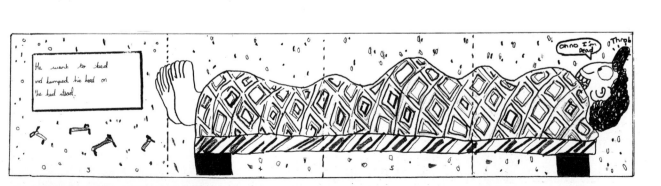

'The Man from Peru' by Louise (11) (artwork on pull out pages 4–6)

Louise discovered that, because of the way the book is folded, page 4–5 can be pulled out as a continuous strip. So already the book's design was making demands on the author. Pages 4, 5 and 6 were therefore designated as a pull-out illustration and the remaining pages were allocated roles as shown – four story and six illustration pages. From the first encounter, it was clear that Louise was going to approach the book in a humorous vein. 'What a crazy book!' she said, and who could disagree with her?

'The Man from Peru' uses rhyme to propel the imagery along.

(1) There was a man from Peru/Who lived on a lou (sic). (3) He went to bed and bumped his head on the bedstead. (7) He dreamed about getting wed. (9) And woke up thinking he was dead.
    All this was composed alongside the empty book format, so that corresponding rough draft pages were prepared for writing and graphic work. The idea of pages 4–6 containing a bed prompted the head/bedstead rhyme. The style of graphic, comic strip imagery has come from popular publishing, but the iconic forms are never stereotypical: they manage to be alive and personal. We discussed design and layout – assymetric balance of words and images and ways of organising the book's design. So the book came into being in stage by stage transfers from final draft to book presentation. The completed book was given a thin white card wrap around cover.

Wrap around cover design

Beginning of story

We discussed design and layout

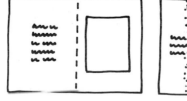
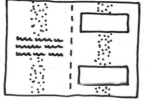
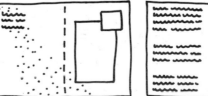

⑰ Book in three parts

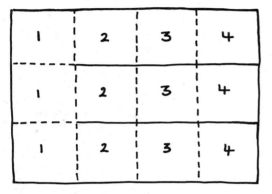

A2   3×4

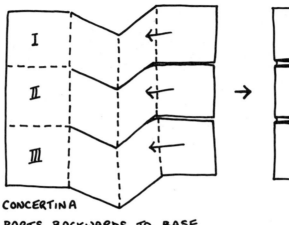

CONCERTINA
PARTS BACKWARDS TO BASE.

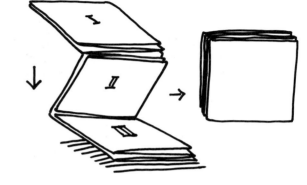

CONCERTINA THREE SECTIONS
DOWNWARDS.

Cut-out book illustration (student)

Another cutting pattern on the same 3 × 4 fold produces a book in three pull-out sections.

It is so easy for children's illustrative and design work to be limited to pen and pencil work. Always employing examples of excellence from the commercial presses in my teaching, I used for this project Jan Pienkowski's beautifully designed *Easter* (Heinemann, 1989) with black cut-out illustrations.

Nick (10) liked doing cartoon-type drawings, but for his book I persuaded him to have a go at silhouette figures in black paper. The more he investigated the technique, the deeper his involvement in the mysterious visual power of the solid black image on white, as his work will

testify. This is another example of the intuitive sense of design that children have. How well the shapes and 'psychological relationships' of the figures and objects exist in the spatial field of the page. So Nick found in front of him a three part book waiting to be transformed into a story. The synopsis of his story is as follows: Nick is sent out shopping and sees what he believes to be a dead body but it turns out to be a coat. In his excitement he forgets what he is sent out for and returns home empty handed.

As he prepared the story for the book he found that it fitted more naturally into three sequences of three. His solution to this was to fill the last panel of each part with a white on black motif.

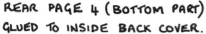

PULL
UPWARDS

1.

GLUE

PART NUMBERS
WRITTEN
ON THE BACK
OF WHITE
ON BLACK
SILHOUETTES.

PULL
UPWARDS

1.

2.

3.

COVER

'Going to the shops' by Nick (10)

A development of the basic origami and multi-fold concertina book is the Tall Story Book. This comprises horizontally-folded A3 divided into six parts.

The format gives an elongated page shape, hence the title. The special feature of the design is that page 5 tucks back to allow the open top fold (6) to fold around it. This produces an open-up section of three pages: 6,7,8. In the prescribed book, a simple recognisable shape is drawn on page 6 which is then continued on the other two adjacent flaps (7,8) by the author. The challenge here is for the author to invent the continuation from page 6 – to the beginning, and the end!

Robin's 'Raiders of the Best Museum' was preoccupied with Tutankhamen when this 'Tall Book' project began and so he adapted the format to accommodate the topic of the ancient Egyptians. Again the style of writing and graphic presentation has been influenced by strip cartoons. The prepared image on page 6 is conceived as a rock, although the reader is led to believe it is a bone. By setting the story around the disappearance of Tutankhamen's left elbow bone from a museum invites reader participation: 'Can you guess what the picture on page 6 is? Turn the page and find out.'

Pages 9–11 conclude the story by the protagonist 'Super Pharoah' returning the bone to the museum.

A3

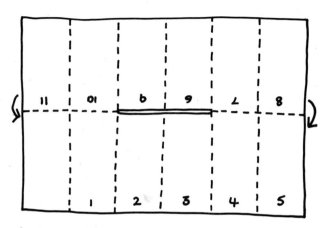

FOLD DOWN.

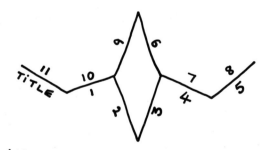

PLAN.

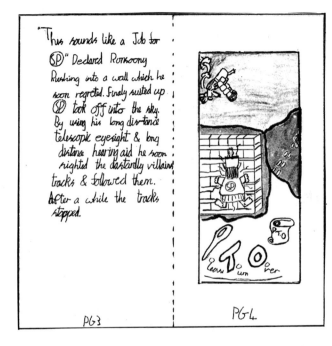

Page from 'Raiders of the Best Museum' by Robin (9)

The challenge for the reader is to guess what the continued form is before opening the flaps 7 and 8. This feature is the pivotal point of the book for the image conceived diverts the story forward to page 1 and to page 11.

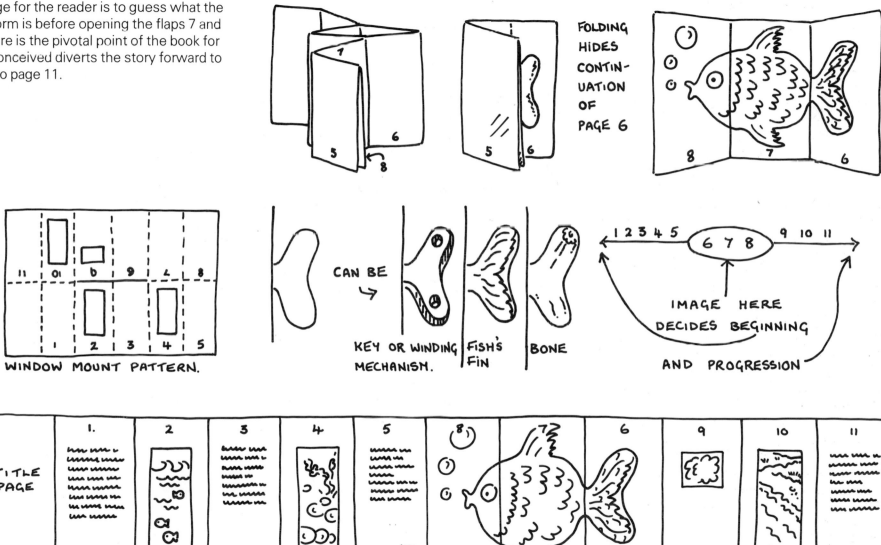

FOLDING HIDES CONTINUATION OF PAGE 6

PLAN

WINDOW MOUNT PATTERN.

CAN BE →

KEY OR WINDING MECHANISM.

FISH'S FIN

BONE

1 2 3 4 5   6 7 8   9 10 11

IMAGE HERE DECIDES BEGINNING

AND PROGRESSION

TITLE PAGE

1.

2

3

4

5

6

9

10

11

Because of the design of the central image, pages 6, 7 and 8 run in reverse to the chronological order. Pages for writing are faced with illustration pages with additional pages for either writing or images.

Binding – The title is hinged to the inside front of a wrap around cover. All the other pages need to be left free so there is no back page attachment.

Illustrations from Robin's book showing the opening out 6–8 sequence

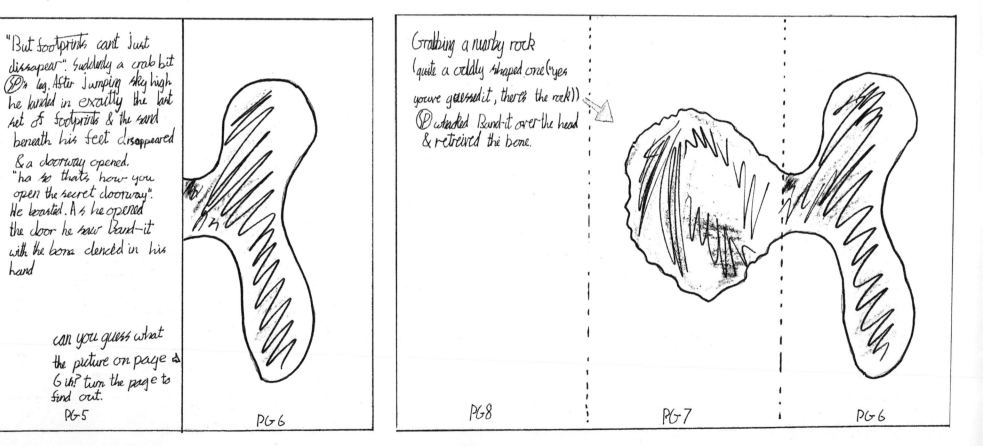

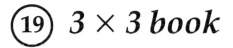
This book is the result of another experiment with paper cutting and folding. A door has been cut into one of the folds and then the sheet is concertina-folded as shown.

Adele turned the pages of her ready-made book and decided on the front as title page, pages 1, 2 and 3 as story, but then she puzzled over the remaining three pages because they were all joined together. We discussed possible ways of using this in her story but, as so often happens, the 'door' symbol took charge of her thinking and these pages portrayed a series of doors leading, in effect, out of the book. Working backwards from these doors into the story, she was required to devise a plot on three, approximately 15 cm square pages. Her idea of John tyring to escape from the book is carefully constructed to fit the dimensions of the pages.

The finished book was bound into a simple wrap around cover and a fourth door cut into the back, enabling John to finally escape.

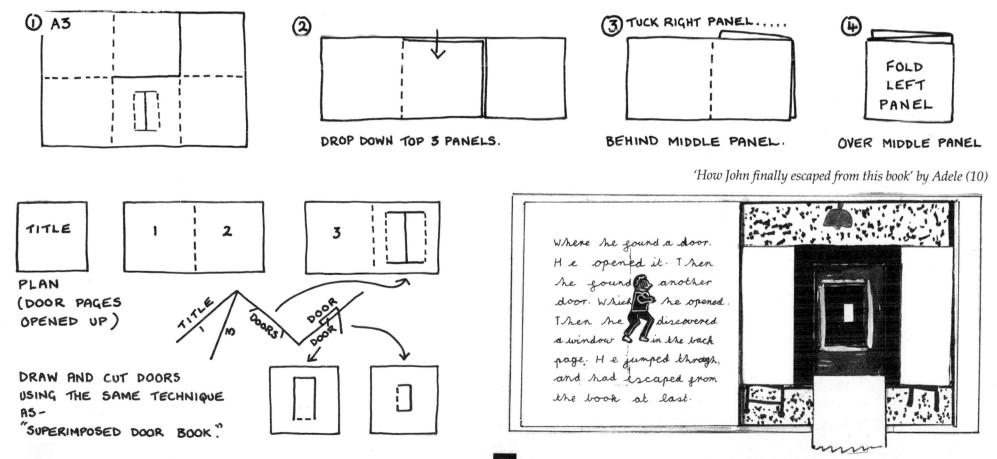

① **A3**

② DROP DOWN TOP 3 PANELS.

③ TUCK RIGHT PANEL......
BEHIND MIDDLE PANEL.

④ FOLD LEFT PANEL
OVER MIDDLE PANEL

'How John finally escaped from this book' by Adele (10)

TITLE · 1 · 2 · 3

PLAN
(DOOR PAGES
OPENED UP)

DRAW AND CUT DOORS
USING THE SAME TECHNIQUE
AS –
"SUPERIMPOSED DOOR BOOK."

TITLE 1 3 DOORS DOOR DOOR

Where he found a door. He opened it. Then he found another door. Which he opened. Then he discovered a window in the back page. He jumped through, and had escaped from the book at last.

(20) *Book with pop-up*

This is one of the first experimental books I made from a single sheet of paper, and it has remained one of the most popular with children.

Stage 1

① A2

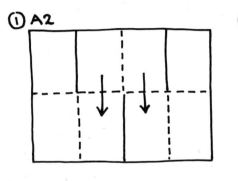

②

B A
B B A A

DROP TOP MIDDLE FLAP FORWARDS.

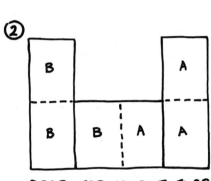

③ FOLD 'A' OVER 'B'.
FOLD OUTER FLAPS TOWARDS CENTRE.

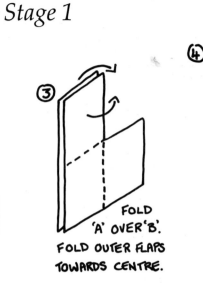

④ DROP TOP SINGLE FLAPS DOWN. TURN TO HORIZONTAL POSITION.

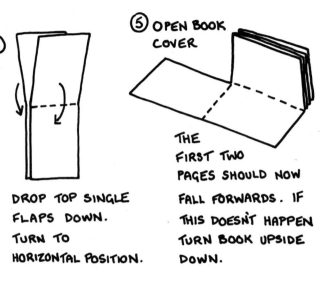

⑤ OPEN BOOK COVER

THE FIRST TWO PAGES SHOULD NOW FALL FORWARDS. IF THIS DOESN'T HAPPEN TURN BOOK UPSIDE DOWN.

Stage 2

ORDERING PAGE SEQUENCE

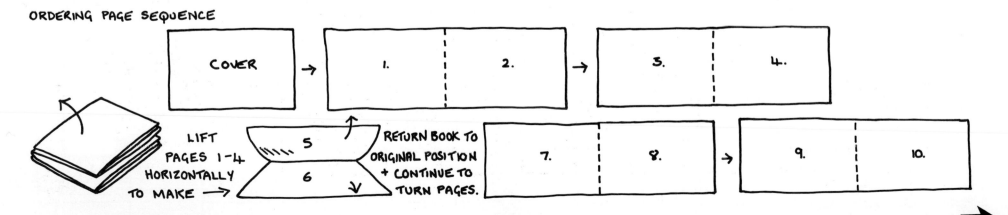

COVER → | 1. | 2. | → | 3. | 4. |

LIFT PAGES 1-4 HORIZONTALLY TO MAKE →

5 / 6

RETURN BOOK TO ORIGINAL POSITION + CONTINUE TO TURN PAGES.

| 7. | 8. | → | 9. | 10. |

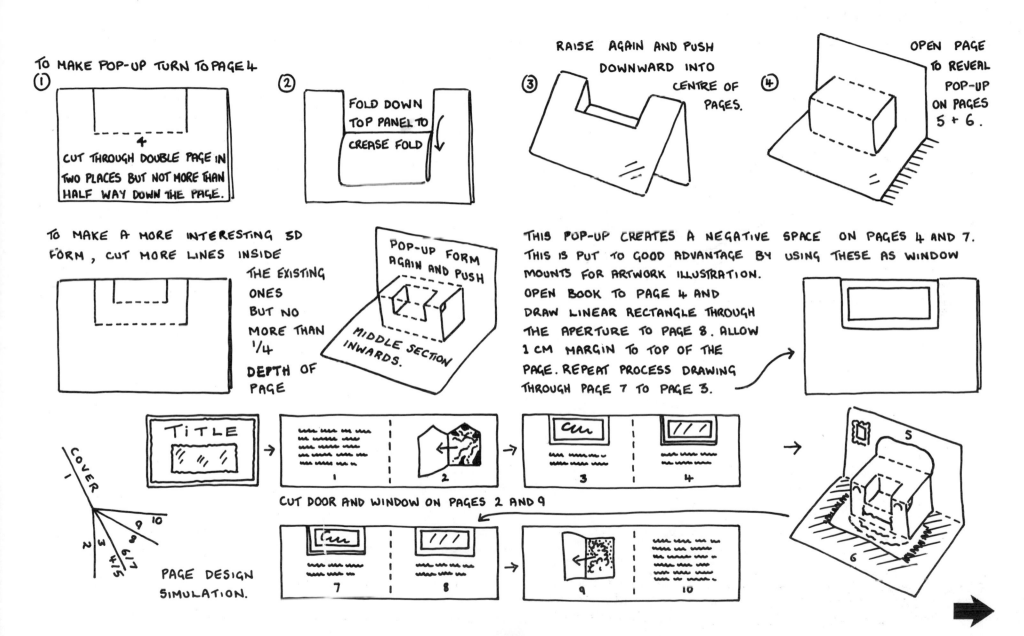

TO MAKE POP-UP TURN TO PAGE 4
① CUT THROUGH DOUBLE PAGE IN TWO PLACES BUT NOT MORE THAN HALF WAY DOWN THE PAGE.

② FOLD DOWN TOP PANEL TO CREASE FOLD

③ RAISE AGAIN AND PUSH DOWNWARD INTO CENTRE OF PAGES.

④ OPEN PAGE TO REVEAL POP-UP ON PAGES 5 + 6.

TO MAKE A MORE INTERESTING 3D FORM, CUT MORE LINES INSIDE THE EXISTING ONES BUT NO MORE THAN 1/4 DEPTH OF PAGE

POP-UP FORM AGAIN AND PUSH MIDDLE SECTION INWARDS.

THIS POP-UP CREATES A NEGATIVE SPACE ON PAGES 4 AND 7. THIS IS PUT TO GOOD ADVANTAGE BY USING THESE AS WINDOW MOUNTS FOR ARTWORK ILLUSTRATION. OPEN BOOK TO PAGE 4 AND DRAW LINEAR RECTANGLE THROUGH THE APERTURE TO PAGE 8. ALLOW 1 CM MARGIN TO TOP OF THE PAGE. REPEAT PROCESS DRAWING THROUGH PAGE 7 TO PAGE 3.

COVER

PAGE DESIGN SIMULATION.

TITLE

CUT DOOR AND WINDOW ON PAGES 2 AND 9

The book is almost mirror-imaged, the pop-up middle section being the pivot. The number of writing lines to each page depends upon the stage of development of the children. For a class of six- or seven-year-olds one or two lines might represent an acceptable number of words, whereas a whole page of writing might be expected of top juniors. (Of course, quantity does not equate with quality, but I use these as a rough guide when designing writing pages.)

I first explored this book form with a class of year five pupils. Each had a blank book in front of them and we went through my simulation page by page. We discussed what could happen through doors and windows and how these ideas could influence the crafted story. The central pop-up was inevitably the climax and we brainstormed a multitude of things: a cubic form could be a chair, throne, box, car, or house. An unfortunate condition of the pop-up form put to

good use is the negative space it makes. The open area has been utilised as a window for illustrations on pages 3 and 8. This produces the same illustration on page 8 as page 4, and page 7 as page 3. This requires two pieces of artwork to be accommodated by four pieces of writing.

It is a very challenging book form but one to which the children responded at once with excitement. They numbered the pages of their jotters 1–10, corresponding to the book's pages and then set about the rough draft of the story. They were at liberty to illustrate (from rough sketches) at any point during the project.

Some found that the story idea could be conceptualised more clearly by being drawn first, whilst others preferred to complete the writing first. But the general pattern of creative behaviour was for the story drafting/writing and illustration to be processed concurrently. Perhaps the biggest challenge was to provide two illustrations to fit the four pages of writing.

Rough draft jotters correspond to the blank book pages

Panda Bear

One day Panda-Bear was eating his bamboo, Hoot Hoot was near by eating a worm "Munch Munch" As they were eating they heard parrot calling "hey Hoot Hoot parrot is calling" cried Panda Bear, so they ran off to meet him. "Hey parrot" what is it "asked Panda-Bear. Parrot told them that there was a strange door at the west side of the jungle.

Panda-Bear packed a few bamboo canes and off they went. Half way there they stoped for lunch. When they got up it was nearly Noon so they hurried off and they arrived 3 hours later. There in froint of them was a big Red and blue door "shall we go through" said parrot "why not" said panda-Bear!

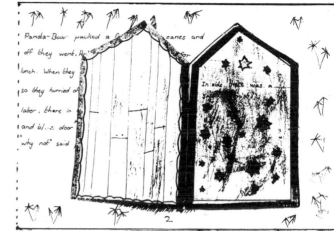

Door open

'Don't Forget the Travelling Pills!!' by Philip (9) is an accomplished realisation of this pop-up story book form. He has an intuitive feeling for words and images, and both grow together on the page effortlessly.

They couldn't believe their eyes they were in the desert. The desert was 9 degrees and only one palm tree in sight. There was sand on sand. Sand every... "hey" cried panda Bear "its to hot lets get out of here. So they ran and ran and ran and soon they came to this window!

A window in the middle of the sky through the window they could see the North pole. They stepped back and fell down this hole.

Pop-up
(flat position)

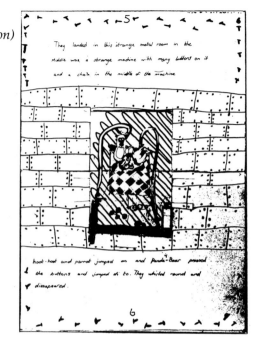

Philip uses the window on page 4 to see through to the North Pole on page 8, and the desert island on page 3 is seen through the windows on page 7. He exploits these dual images expressively by glueing a window frame to the negative pop-up space; one sees what is to be in the future and what has been in the past.

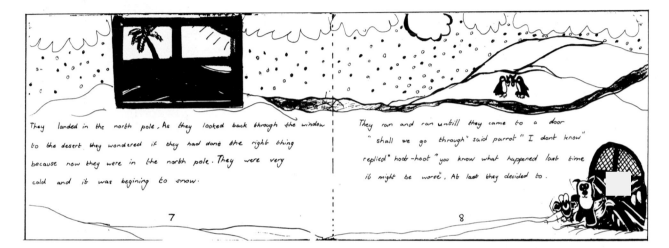

Door open

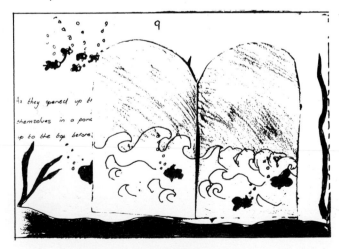

Flat pieces of paper made into environmental books are many in number. Two are described. The artwork and writing has to be done in the flat state so the positioning of rooms, inside and out, and placing of writing must be marked on the sheet before commencing work.

The design presents three inside and three outside walls of the room and four pages of writing.

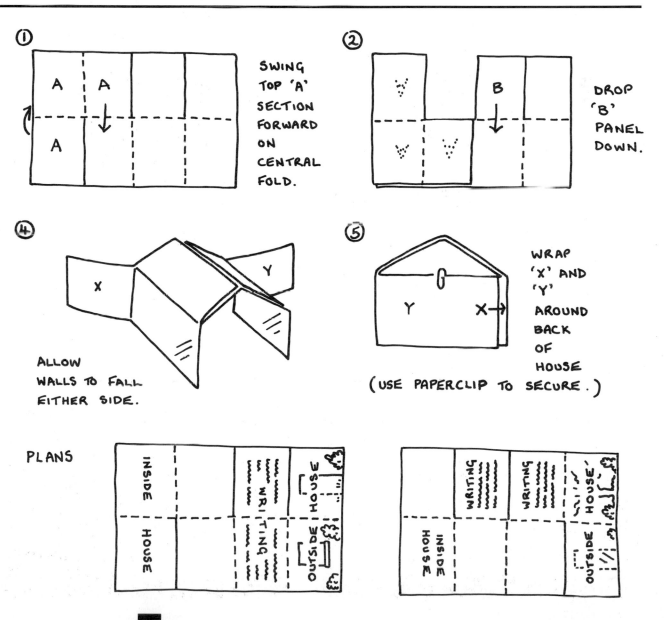

① SWING TOP 'A' SECTION FORWARD ON CENTRAL FOLD.

② DROP 'B' PANEL DOWN.

③ LIFT ✳ TO CREATE ROOF

④ ALLOW WALLS TO FALL EITHER SIDE.

⑤ WRAP 'X' AND 'Y' AROUND BACK OF HOUSE (USE PAPERCLIP TO SECURE.)

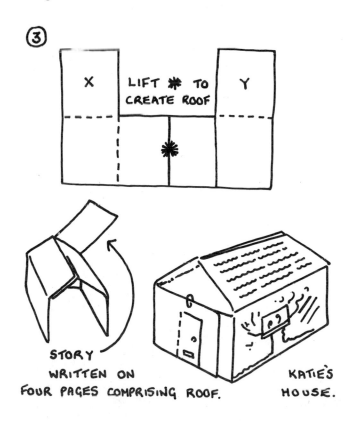

STORY WRITTEN ON FOUR PAGES COMPRISING ROOF.

KATIE'S HOUSE.

PLANS

This method produces a three-dimensional theatre with five pages for writing/illustration on the rear panel.

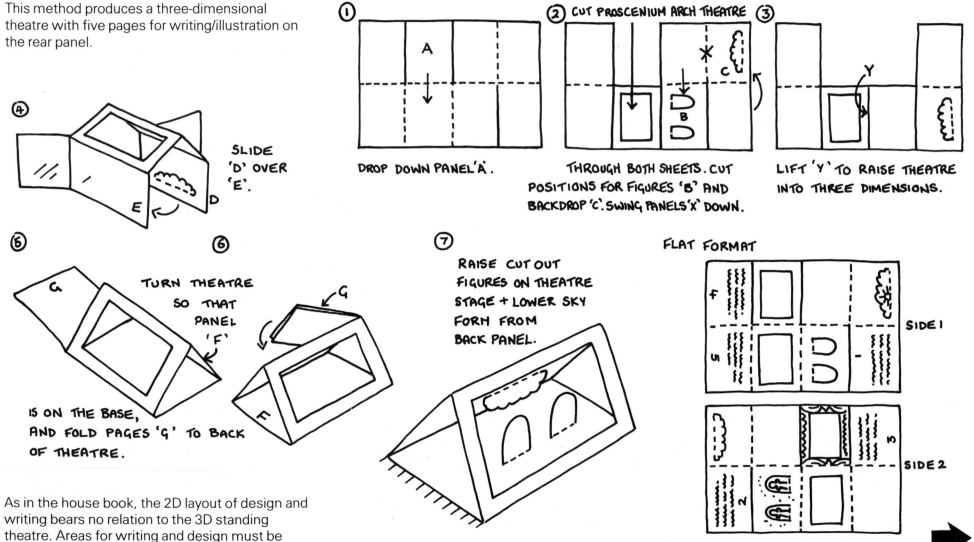

① DROP DOWN PANEL 'A'.

② CUT PROSCENIUM ARCH THEATRE
THROUGH BOTH SHEETS. CUT POSITIONS FOR FIGURES 'B' AND BACKDROP 'C'. SWING PANELS 'X' DOWN.

③ LIFT 'Y' TO RAISE THEATRE INTO THREE DIMENSIONS.

④ SLIDE 'D' OVER 'E'.

⑤ TURN THEATRE SO THAT PANEL 'F' IS ON THE BASE, AND FOLD PAGES 'G' TO BACK OF THEATRE.

⑥

⑦ RAISE CUT OUT FIGURES ON THEATRE STAGE + LOWER SKY FORM FROM BACK PANEL.

FLAT FORMAT

SIDE 1

SIDE 2

As in the house book, the 2D layout of design and writing bears no relation to the 3D standing theatre. Areas for writing and design must be prepared on the flat format.

Nicola's 'Theatre Story' is a rhyming satire on Romeo and Juliet. Romeo is so small he has to stand on chairs, and Juliet is a kind of punk with bright pink hair. If they make a mistake a trap door opens beneath them, and they fall through to wild animals.

The scene through the proscenium arch shows the two performers on the raised (puppet) panels whilst the animals are drawn through the negative shapes on the base panel. The story on the five outer pages is carefully arranged on the page, and is balanced by the humorous accompanying drawings. Additionally, Nicola has added a moveable paper curtain to the front of the theatre.

'Theatre Story, by Nicola (10)

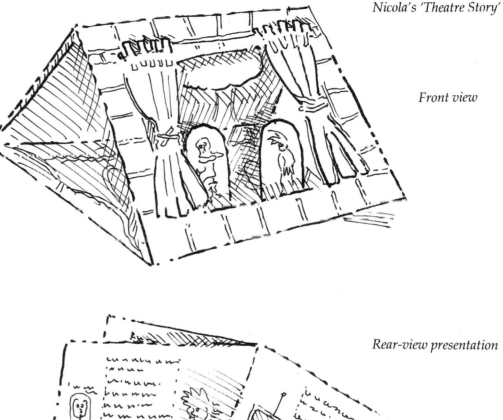

Nicola's 'Theatre Story'

Front view

Rear-view presentation

There once was a group called plays,
They did there plays in funny ways
The latest one there going to do,
Is one I've heard of so most you
Romeo and Juliet is the name,
Romeo's small and Juliet's called Jane
Poor Romeo he is so small,
He has to stand on chairs and stools
If someone makes a small mistake,
They fall through a trap door and used
As bait.

(23) *Peep show book*

Another 3D book, but of a much simpler kind, returns to the diminishing door theme.

When the concertina doors are stood on end vertically and pulled down over page 4 of the bottom concertina, a vista is created through the arcade of openings.

Andrew (8) has exploited this 'peep show' effect to good use in his book 'Treasure in the House of Horrors'. Here, the diminishing doors revealed what appeared to be a sports car, but on closer inspection turned out to be a cannon.

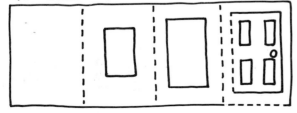

TOP LINE ARTWORK (BACK VIEW)

TOP LINE ARTWORK (FRONT VIEW)

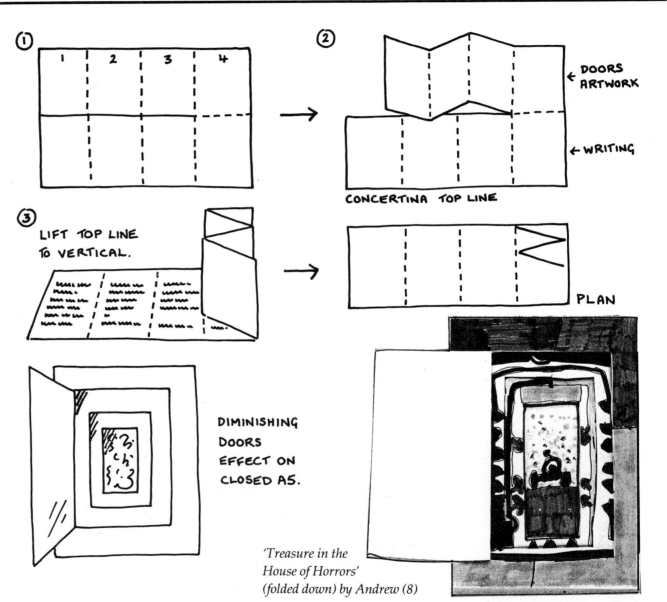

① 1 2 3 4

② DOORS ARTWORK ← WRITING

CONCERTINA TOP LINE

③ LIFT TOP LINE TO VERTICAL.

PLAN

DIMINISHING DOORS EFFECT ON CLOSED A5.

'Treasure in the House of Horrors' (folded down) by Andrew (8)

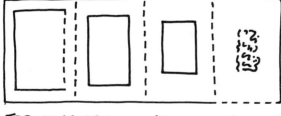

Applied covers for books

1 Basic cover (wrap around)

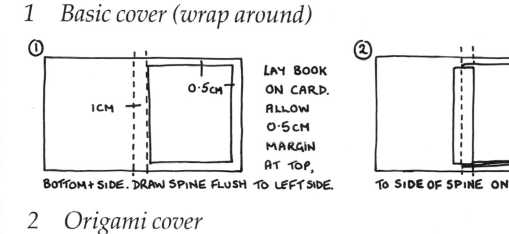

① LAY BOOK ON CARD. ALLOW 0.5CM MARGIN AT TOP, BOTTOM + SIDE. DRAW SPINE FLUSH TO LEFT SIDE.

0.5CM

1CM

② GLUE STRIP TO TITLE PAGE THEN FASTEN TO SIDE OF SPINE ON INSIDE FRONT COVER.

③ ALTERNATIVELY GLUE STRIP TO SPINE.

2 Origami cover

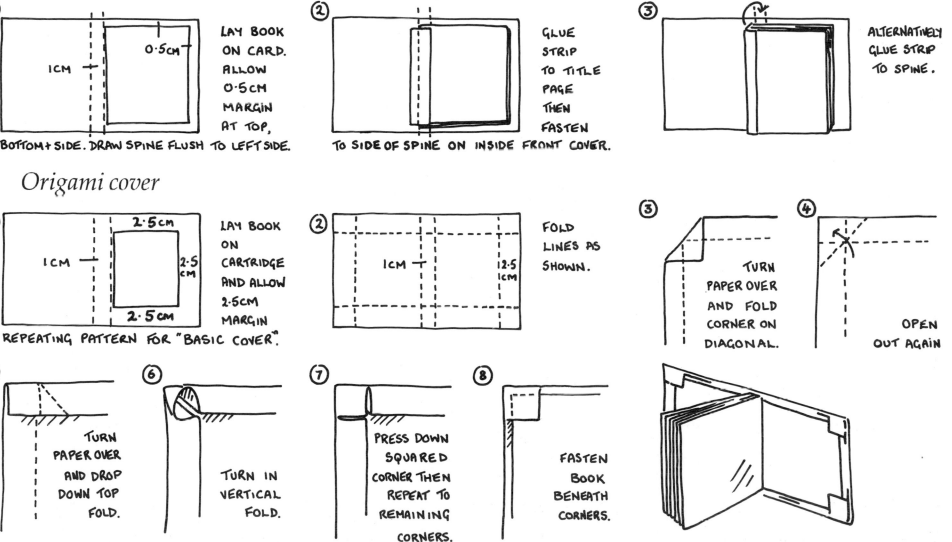

① LAY BOOK ON CARTRIDGE AND ALLOW 2.5CM MARGIN REPEATING PATTERN FOR "BASIC COVER".

2.5CM

1CM

2.5 CM

2.5CM

② FOLD LINES AS SHOWN.

1CM

2.5 1CM

③ TURN PAPER OVER AND FOLD CORNER ON DIAGONAL.

④ OPEN OUT AGAIN

⑤ TURN PAPER OVER AND DROP DOWN TOP FOLD.

⑥ TURN IN VERTICAL FOLD.

⑦ PRESS DOWN SQUARED CORNER THEN REPEAT TO REMAINING CORNERS.

⑧ FASTEN BOOK BENEATH CORNERS.

Drafting books

One of the problems with preparing European, centrally-bound books is that one must calculate the number of pages required in advance of the book's assembly. To add pages to the back in order to continue a story also adds unwanted pages to the front. One of the ways to avoid this is to make a loose-leaf drafting book with slotted pages.

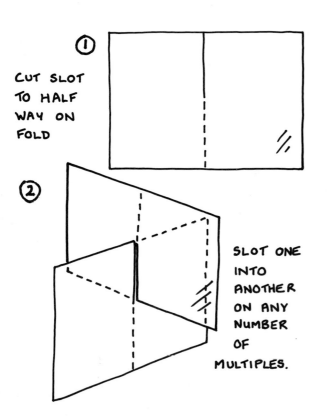

① CUT SLOT TO HALF WAY ON FOLD

② SLOT ONE INTO ANOTHER ON ANY NUMBER OF MULTIPLES.

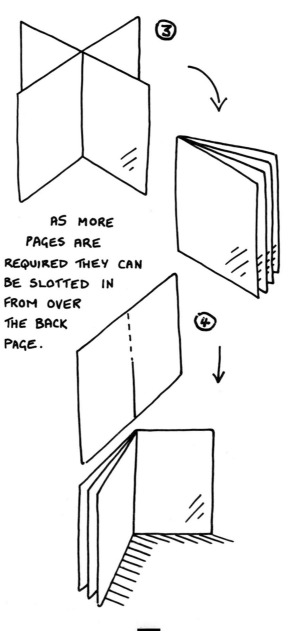

③

④

AS MORE PAGES ARE REQUIRED THEY CAN BE SLOTTED IN FROM OVER THE BACK PAGE.

General notes about folding paper

Folding sheets of paper too many times on top of one another can produce untidy creases. To avoid this the following folding pattern may be useful.

BASIC EIGHT DIVISION FOLD

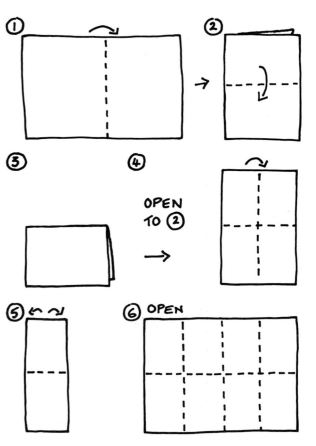

①

②

③

④   OPEN TO ②

⑤   ⑥ OPEN

Folding in threes

FOLDING PAPER INTO 3 EQUAL PARTS CAN BE
IRKSOME – HERE ARE SOME SUGGESTIONS:

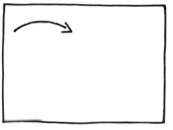

FOLD PAPER
TO MAKE
TWO PANELS
OF 'EYE
MEASURED'
EQUALITY,
PRACTISE EYE
TRAINING IN THIS WAY – WITH
EXPERIENCE YOU WILL BE SURPRISED
HOW ACCURATELY YOU CAN 'EYE
MEASURE '.

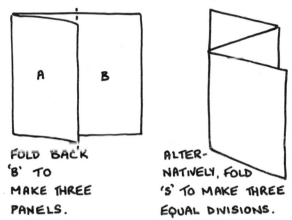

FOLD BACK
'B' TO
MAKE THREE
PANELS.

ALTER-
NATIVELY, FOLD
'S' TO MAKE THREE
EQUAL DIVISIONS.

Publishing one-off books

The beauty and sadness of the one-off book is that it is the only one in the world. Children who make beautiful books find that everyone (headteacher, classteacher, parents, grandmother et al.) wants to own them.

A compromise here, and one which I use regularly, is to photocopy the original. There are some problems, like the poor quality of half-tone reproduction, but these can be overcome by working over the copy in black linework as a master before running more copies off. Another problem is finding centres that can copy and/or reduce from A1/2. But the photocopied book can have a charm all of its own. Some children are more attached to them than to the original!

Books with infants and nursery children

Books with infants

Building up a relationship with young children is essential to their developing the self-assurance to write. Beryl teaches a mixed reception/middle infant class and has done just that by using children's self-made books.

The first book she made with them was a simple folded card with door (these are illustrated on page 30). The children loved these because of the element of surprise and simplicity. She finds the concept of writing a strain for many children. A way around this is to encourage scribble writing to gain

confidence in the pencil and this helps to avoid the break in thought processes which so easily happens when young children start to write. The books Beryl made for them were so exciting to look at that their fear was overcome. In standard writing books they feel compelled to write on and on as if psychologically programmed to 'finish the book'. This is a daunting prospect and turns children off writing. With one-off books the teacher can decide what kind of book and what length of book is most suitable for each child.

From the simple folded card developed the

basic origami book (see page 39). The children were encouraged to draw first so that their illustrations would be a further stimulation to writing. As Beryl says:

> 'Children need to orally communicate their stories without fear of writing expectation by the teacher.'

From the six page origami book evolved the concertina book (see page 24), with its four large format pages.

The children found these exciting, but they still needed to be 'eased' into them from the smaller books they had just finished. To

Contour book by Lindsey (5)

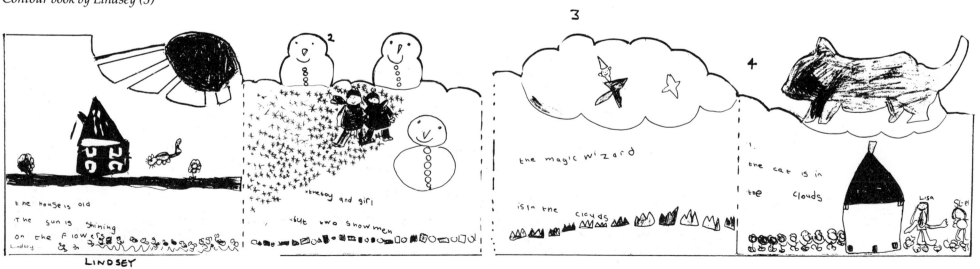

the house is old
The sun is shining
on the flowers
Lindsey
LINDSEY

the boy and girl
but two snowmen

the magic wizard
is in the clouds

the cat is in
the clouds
Lisa Stel

achieve this Beryl designed a cut contour to the four pages. In the first books these were very recognisable shapes. For example, Lindsey's book had:

- sun with rays
- head and shoulder
- cloud
- cat

Lindsey wrote:

(1) the house is old the sun is shining on the flowers

(2) the boy and girl but (sic) two snowmen

(3) the magic wizard is in the clouds

(4) the cat is in the clouds.

With Leeanne's prescribed contours the figuration was less defined as shown below.

Beryl thinks children generally don't enjoy writing:

'They get lost in standard writing books, but their own books make writing enjoyable. Parents can't believe what they've done, and children can't wait to make the next one.'

Leeanne wrote:

(1) Once upon a time there was a magic hill the hill stole all the colours of the rainbow one day the magic hill was ill

(2) the towns never heard about the hill one day the hill went out for a walk the magic hill saw a ghost the hill spoke to the ghost

(3) the hill said who are you the ghost

Leeanne (5)

replied I live in ghost town where is ghost town here whatever are you talking about what does he mean the ghost wasn't looking were he was going and he bumped into a haystack

(4)   and at the back of the haystack there was a muddy old pond the ghost was stuck there for 100 years

There is much greater confidence in (a) the story structure, (b) writing, (c) artwork, (d) total page design. The whole book is a visual delight, an explosion of shapes and colours.

There was a tendency for each panel to be completed in its entirety before moving on to the next one. Children would come to Beryl and seek guidance and reassurance before progessing.

Jennifer's book has vague outlines but by this stage of making books the ability to interpret a shape has advanced.

'and one day they were playing out. One of them said to the other come and play in my house and she had a basket it was brown and it had a black handle with yellow pins . . .'

Between these examples is Mary's in which stars, staircase and windows are clearly delineated by the teacher, but the child has

Jennifer (6)

and one day they were playing out. one of them said to the other come and play in my house and she had a basket it was brown and it had a black handle with yellow pins she has purple wallpaper and then her mum was shouting up to them she was saying to them can you go to the shop and get some food for me we have got no food so they got basket and set off to the shop they were very quick and they got all of the stuff in the basket

When they went to the shops there mum said they could get something for them self and they got some greeps and they did not see a noet that said magic greeps if you eat the greeps you can make a' wish and when they got home they found out that they were magic greeps and they did see the note and they did eat the greeps very quick and they wish to be twins and all of a sudden they were twins.

Mary (6)

it was night and the stars shining but three stars were different one was purple one was red and one was pink

but below the stars there was a field in the field a house was there in the house lived a farmer the farmer had a boy the boy was calld Sam

Sam was looking out of the window he saw the 3 stars he wet up the stairs he took his bag and rushed down and went out

out side on the hill he opened his bag he took out a ladder The ladder went right up to the stars he took the stars and went home

and had tea with his dad alfer a while Sam showed his dad the 3 stars and his dad took them and you usd them to make 3 decorations

extracted more than a basic concept from them.

Lisa's book represents the cut contour technique at its most challenging and productive, for her story covers the eight pages. The shapes correspond to four pages of story matched on the reverse. In each of the pages Lisa has visualised a different situation. The cellar window of page 2 is the centre of the flower of page 7. Descending stairs page 3 – ascending stairs page 6. Three windows of page 4 become trees on page 5.

Another way of continuing the story but without turning the page was invented by Steve (6) who, when reaching page 4

Lisa (6)

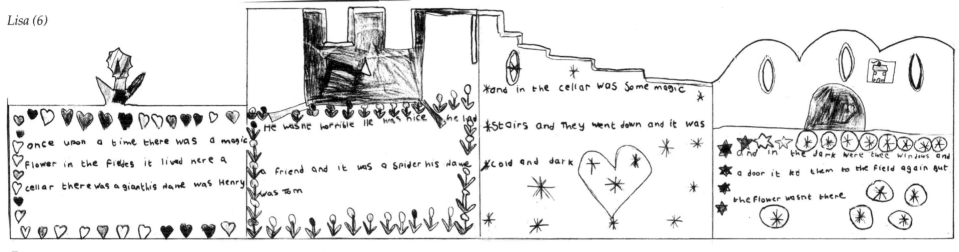

Front

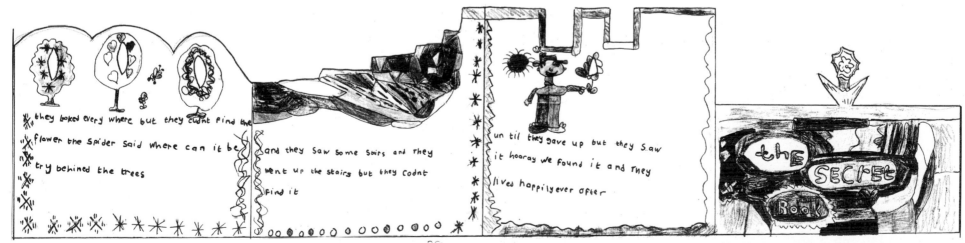

Back

continued the story in an attached origami book.

All these books evolved through the stimulus of the concertina form itself. Without the book and its outlines it is questionable if so much developmental writing would have occurred for, as Beryl said, 'the outline is an aid to discovery'. Beryl's visual aid shows children how cut shapes can tell a story.

'The Two Flying Cars' by Steve (6) illustrates, again, the intuitive sense of design that children have if free to express it in an atmosphere conducive to creativity. The words and images coexist in perfect asymetrical harmony on the page. This book was made on good quality, heavy cartridge paper, and Steve has reciprocated quality of

paper with quality of work. Could anything like this have been produced in a tatty exercise book? The reward for so much effort was for Beryl to bind the book using hard covers which Steve ultimately furnished with a cover design.

Finally, two side-bound books. (For details of this technique see p.98.)

'The Castle Book' by Rachel (5) is an illustrated story in six pages and in 'The Butterfly Book, by Lisa (5) the illustrations and text have been made on separate pieces of paper and glued in. This is an excellent approach for children who need to write 'as the spirit moves them' without the prescription of a set number of pages. For the

Steve (6)–Page 4 showing origami book on bottom right side of page

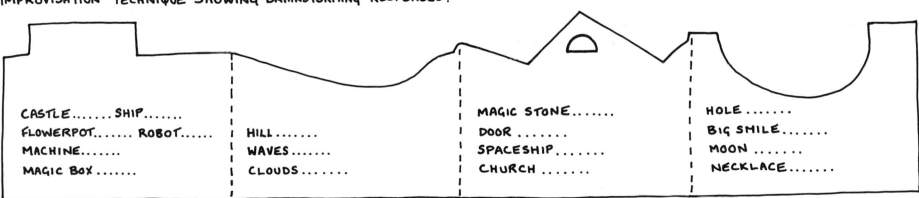

IMPROVISATION TECHNIQUE SHOWING BRAINSTORMING RESPONSES.

CASTLE....... SHIP.......
FLOWERPOT....... ROBOT......
MACHINE.......
MAGIC BOX.......

HILL.......
WAVES.......
CLOUDS.......

MAGIC STONE.......
DOOR.......
SPACESHIP.......
CHURCH.......

HOLE.......
BIG SMILE.......
MOON.......
NECKLACE.......

BERYL'S VISUAL AID SHOWS CHILDREN HOW CUT SHAPES CAN TELL A STORY.

less confident child the artwork and writing glued down one piece at a time is a stepping-stone process, building confidence in writing. Later, Lisa was confident enough to make a whole book working directly on to the paper. (Both books were bound by the class teacher.)

These few examples show how an imaginative teacher can build confidence in writing skills through the concrete stimulation of the book form.

'The Castle Book' by Rachel (5)

'The Butterfly Book' by Lisa (5)

Books in the nursery

These books by four-year-olds illustrate how the concertina fold presentation can enable even very young children to sequence their thinking and image making.

Jacqueline's 'the cat is sitting down' (picture 1) is a simple one-fold form showing imagery on all four surfaces.

In Heather's book (picture 2), the four-phase sequence shows (*a*) Heather; (*b*) her Mummy and Daddy; (*c*) having tea – milk jug; (*d*) teapot (a 'flowered' teapot).

David's 'story' (picture 3) shows (*d*) 'me'; (*b*) 'taking a doggy for a walk'. It is interesting to observe that although there is perceived a chronological sequence, it does not necessarily move in a left to right direction.

Sacha said of his story (picture 4) 'This is a man going for a walk through some trees and he sees a monster who chases him.'

This three-sequence story (picture 5), produced on a single origami book structure, shows clearly how the prescribed form has projected a forward development of imagery. From (*a*) isolated house, to (*b*) house with garden, to (*c*) 'me standing by my house'.

Finally, Samantha's retelling of Goldilocks (picture 6) sequences the story for her in a visually controlled evolution of images.

Nursery children at work on their books

①

Cover   *Inside*

② *a*   *b*   *c*   *d*

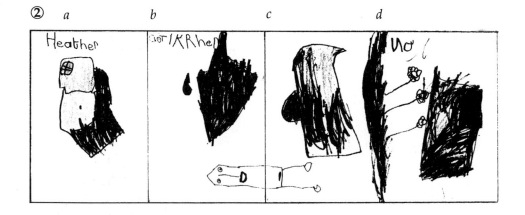

③ *a*   *b*   *c*   *d*

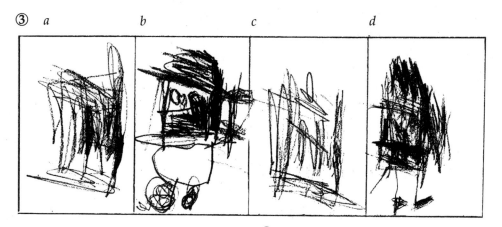

④

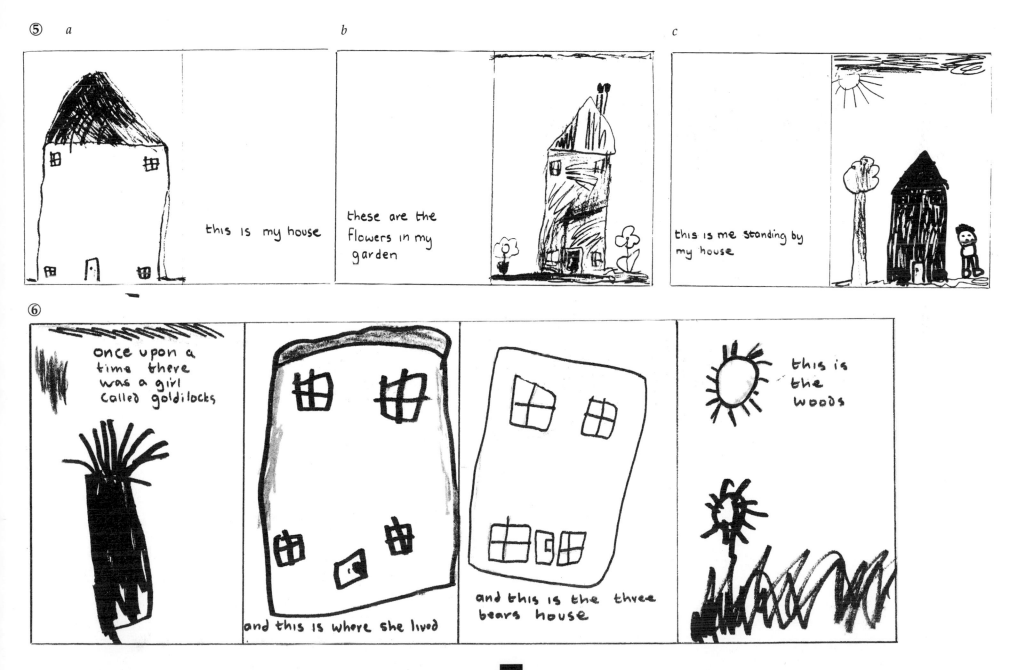

⑤   *a*   *b*   *c*

this is my house

these are the flowers in my garden

this is me standing by my house

⑥

once upon a time there was a girl called goldilocks

and this is where she lived

and this is the three bears house

this is the woods

6 *A Book of many styles*

This book concept was the result of a project with thirty-two year four pupils. The aim was to develop several different writing styles incorporated into one collective book. It was divided into eight parts for no other reason than that it fitted equally into the class size. In practice, the distribution of eight tasks was not rigidly adhered to, some pupils preferring alternative strategies.

The objective was to use the story form as the catalyst for styles of writing not normally associated with fiction but which, nevertheless, fitted strategically into it. The synopsis of the prescribed story was as follows:

A child sees a poster advertising an exhibition of a valuable object. On visiting the exhibition the child sees thieves steal the object. A newspaper reports the theft. The gallery offers a reward. The child writes to the gallery to report what he saw. This is announced over the radio as a newsflash. The child remembers a vital clue to the thieves' identities and whereabouts. They are arrested. The child uses the reward money to have a holiday.

The division of activities:

The extra activities required to complete the book were done by members of each group as they completed initial work. This was sometimes a joint effort.

Classroom tables were rearranged to accommodate groups of eight and an object placed in the centre. These objects were brought from home and comprised various pieces of valueless objets d'art. They were colourful, small, but large enough for everyone in the group to see clearly. Some children had writing or artwork only roles, whilst others had joint writing/design roles. The visual work was of three kinds: (*i*) observational, based on the objects; (*ii*) imaginative, illustrative, pertaining to the story; (*iii*) layout, design tasks.

Task description

1 *Poster design* This involved selecting information appropriate to the exhibition. Brevity was essential. Artwork of precious object an important part of the design, as was total arrangement of words and images on page.
2 *Story Part I* From child seeing poster to witnessing theft.
3 *Newspaper article* Headline caption, reported account of theft.
4 *Reward poster* Similar to 1, selecting relevant information, artwork, design.
5 *Letter and envelope* Child writes to gallery explaining what he/she saw. Design of envelope, stamp, franking.
6 *Broadcast newsflash* TV/radio reports Police now have a clue to identity of thieves.
7 *Story Part II* Child remembers vital clue which takes him/her to a local shop where thieves are. Reports this to police. Thieves arrested.
8 *Illustration for 7 above* These last two roles are inter-changeable. Extra writing/ illustration could be added if necessary.

Extra tasks

9 *Postcard* Child sends postcard home from holiday. Side A, picture of holiday. Side B, message home. Stamp, franking. Task for one or two children working on either side of postcard. (Two sheets glued together if working in pairs.)
10 *Title page* Design of title, author, artwork.
11 *Cover* Title design and artwork – strip for spine title.
12 *Synopsis* Written precis of story as book page advertisement for book. Copyright information, date of publication.

Blackboard diagram

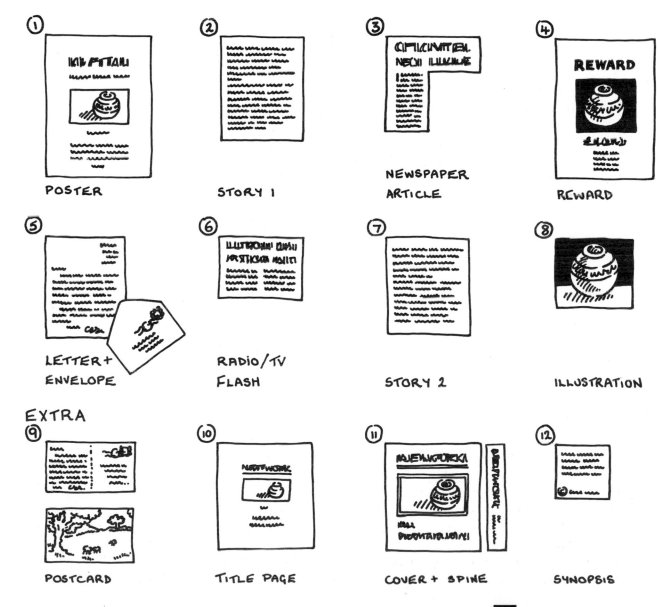

① POSTER

② STORY 1

③ NEWSPAPER ARTICLE

④ REWARD

⑤ LETTER + ENVELOPE

⑥ RADIO/TV FLASH

⑦ STORY 2

⑧ ILLUSTRATION

EXTRA

⑨ POSTCARD

⑩ TITLE PAGE

⑪ COVER + SPINE

⑫ SYNOPSIS

As a stimulus I showed the class *The Jolly Postman* by Janet and Allan Ahlberg (Heinemann, 1986), a delightfully original storybook including lift-out letters throughout. I had explained to them the basic eight-part story structure, with visual references made to the blackboard diagram. A brainstorming episode explained various ways in which the precious object could be stolen, who stole it, how the thieves could be traced, what clues they left behind and how they might be apprehended. Defining the precious object required another improvisation period. The blanks for finished work were distributed to the 4 × 8 children groups.

1 and 4 – comprised A3 cartridge paper.
2 and 7 – paper for story (slightly smaller than A4).
3 – newspaper article in right-angled shape. Horizontal top for headline caption, bottom rectangle for article.
5 – A4 letter and ready-made envelope
6 – paper for newsflash.
8 – cartridge square (15 cm) for illustration.

Postcard – large postcard format, 10–12 prepared similarly from cartridge.

(All the above sizes were designed to fit the proportions of the A2 (3 × 2) book pages.)

These blanks were placed in front of them as aids to visualising the task. Rough paper for writing, design and artwork drafting was also provided along with art materials – a range of pens, crayons, pencil crayons.

Group discussion was encouraged. For example, the name of the object had to be agreed before most participants could commence drafting. The story I (picture 2) was crucial to newspaper article (picture 3), and the revelations of the letter (picture 5) conditioned the newsflash (picture 6), story II (picture 7), and the illustration (picture 8).

The drafting process also had to take into account the shape and size of the master blanks. Too few words would leave an empty space; too many words wouldn't fit.

Towards the end of the first drafting period, the groups read their work (or showed illustrations) to the rest. This enabled the cohesion of the contrasting styles to be tested. Some rewriting became necessary at this stage.

Some of the tasks required special skills, for example poster, reward designs, letter writing and envelope addressing format. For this purpose visual aids were prepared which indicated these requirements. The drafting and collaborative process enabled all the children in the group to experience writing and design styles other than their own. This was important otherwise each child would only have become familiar with one style of writing presentation. An alternative strategy to this group method, and one appropriate to older children, would be for each child to make their own book of many styles of writing.

The task of the final presentation of work on the master blanks was the major activity for

① *Exhibition poster*

② *Story 1*

the second part of the project. Those who finished first moved on to tasks 9–12. The completed work was housed in a book designed to accommodate them. This was done by cutting slots on folded pages through which the material could be slotted (1, 3, 4, 5, 9). And uncut pages were prepared for glued-down work (2, 6, 7, 8, 10, 11).

The reader can imagine the fun and excitement of 'journeying' through the book – taking out folded posters, reading newspaper articles and postcards, opening envelopes. It is not surprising that the whole class asked if they could start a new one right away!

STOLEN MULTI-COLOURED LIQUORICE

On Wednesday 24th May in between 12 and 1 p.m. two people, a man and a woman escaped out of the Whitworth Art Gallery with the Ancient Multi-Coloured Liquorice made by the egyptians. If you think you can describe these people please contact Whitworth Art Gallery or phone 483-6956

③ *Newspaper article*

Reward

Whitworth Art Gallery offers £ 100.000 pounds for the recovery of the ancient egyptians multi coloured Liquorice. If you have seen it call 48366

④ *Reward poster*

3 Adria road
Didsbury
Manchester
M 20 0SQ
24th May 89

Dear Director,
        I saw a man and a woman take the multicoloured liquorice. Between 12:00am and 1.00pm. They put it in a sweet Shop bag. I Followed them and they saw me. But I know where they are.
              yours faithfully
        P.S.   Tom Farra"
              i will tell where they are.

The Director
Whitworth Art Gallery
Oxford rd
Manchester.

⑤ *Letter and envelope*

BBC NEWS

We interrupt tonights exciting ball game to bring you further commentary on the theft of some ancient valuable liquorice from Whitworth Art Gallery in Manchester. The liquorice made by the ancient Egyptians has achieved its different colours by Juices from assorted trees in Egypt. It was layed in a Jeweled case and forgotten about for hundreds of years. It was found in the coffin of king Zilk and is worth £100,000. Just today Witkworth had a letter from a boy called Tom Farra saying that he saw two people steal the ancient multi coloured liquorice and has helped the police enormously with their enquiries. So thankyou Tom and thankyou for watching BBC News

goodbye.

⑥ *Radio/TV newsflash*

Tom was trying to remember what the man and the woman had with them. they had a bag with them but he couldn't remember what it had on the bag. He crossed the road and saw a sweet shop. It was Charlies sweet shop. then he rembered the man and the woman were holding a bag with Charlies sweet shop on it. He ran into the shop and saw the man and woman with the stolen object he sprinted down the street to the nearest phone box and dialed 999. About 5minute's later he heard the siren. He looked down the road and saw the police car. He shouted at the police to stop their car. So they stopied the car, arrested the theives and gave Tom £100,000 and Tom went on Holiday.

⑦ *Story 2*

4p 9p £1.60 Sweet SHOP Multi coloured liquorice £4.8 Frozen Compartment Chocolate Cake Fudge Fire EXIT

⑧ *Illustration*

Dear Mum and Dad

I'm having a brill time in Crete. Its absolutely scorching The hotel that I am staying in has an outdoor swimming pool I have had a swim in it once. It is lovely. The food is delicious especially the wine. I have met a boy called Jack we have been exploring together. I am looking forward to seeing you.

Lots of Love From

Tomxx

P.S. The sun has made me really brown.

Mr & Mrs Farra

3 Adria Road Didsbury Manchester M20 0SQ

ENGLAND

⑨ *Postcard*

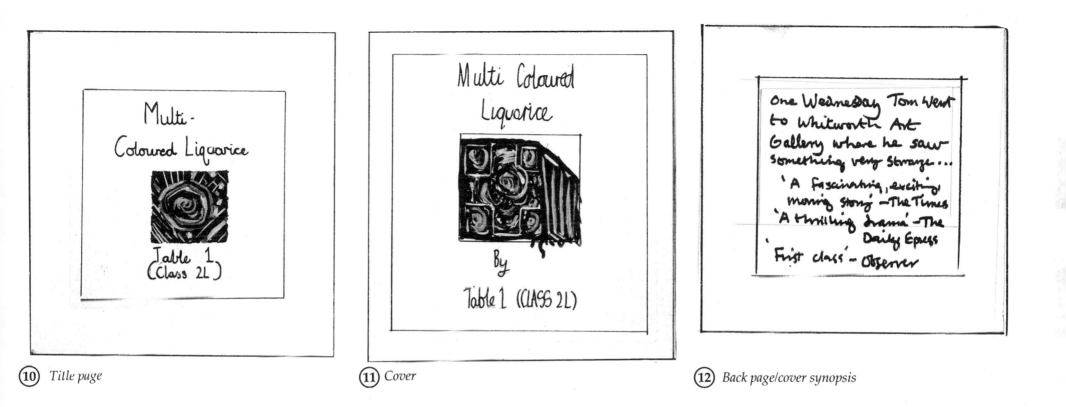

10 *Title page*

11 *Cover*

12 *Back page/cover synopsis*

Book format

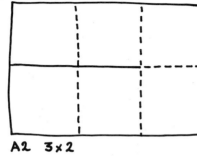

A2   3×2

FOLD AS ABOVE ↑

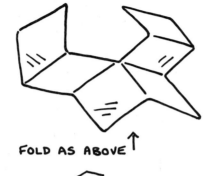

JOIN BOTH A2 SECTIONS
WITH STRIP.
ADD SIMILAR STRIPS
TO BOTH ENDS OF BOOK
TO JOIN COVER.

TITLE   1   2   3   4   5   6   7   8   9   10   11

PLAN

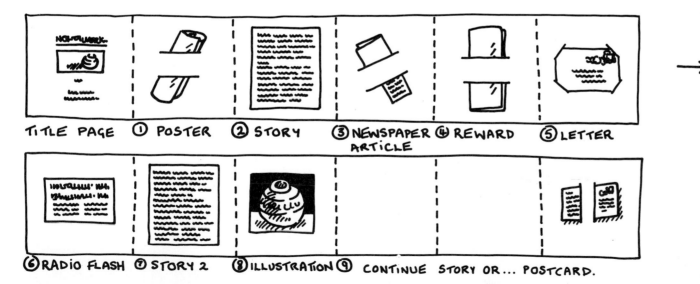

TITLE PAGE   ① POSTER   ② STORY   ③ NEWSPAPER ④ REWARD   ⑤ LETTER
                                      ARTICLE

⑥ RADIO FLASH   ⑦ STORY 2   ⑧ ILLUSTRATION ⑨ CONTINUE STORY OR... POSTCARD.

CUT SLOTS IN PAGES
TO HOLD DETACHED
WORK — POSTER,
NEWSPAPER ARTICLE,
REWARD, LETTER,
POSTCARD.

BASIC WRAP AROUND COVER.

Fastening book to cover

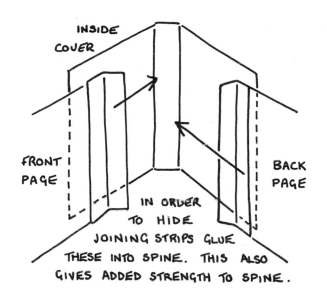

INSIDE COVER

FRONT PAGE

BACK PAGE

IN ORDER TO HIDE JOINING STRIPS GLUE THESE INTO SPINE. THIS ALSO GIVES ADDED STRENGTH TO SPINE.

Crystal Palace

by Class 2L

Palace of Peking

Class 2L

The Mystery of the Disappearing Gobbstoppers

By Class 2L

7 *Group and individual books*

During a visit to Queen's Road Primary School I met Gwen, who teaches Class 10 – a mixed five and six year junior class – and she took me across the playground to her mobile classroom. The small space was packed with children in school uniform and Gwen had asked them to make display labels with their names on, placed on the tables so that I could address them personally. After a brief introduction, during which I showed them different kinds of children's illustrated books, I turned to my ritualistic improvised story. It went something like this:

(Give me an object) A square (A square what?) A box (Can someone give me a rectangle?) A brick. (Now what's different about this brick?) It's soft. (And its colour?) Pink. (So we have a soft brick. Who owns it?) Mark (What did he do with it?) He threw it through a school window. (A soft brick through a window?) It was soft glass. (Then something amazing happened to the brick – what was it?) It was taken aboard Concorde. (I want this story to be more interesting than just an ordinary Concorde . . .) A special interplanetary concorde. (And how does this fit with the soft pink brick in the classroom?) This superhuman concorde was collecting all the soft bricks of the world and taking them to another planet called Redegon. (And what about Mark?) He was taken too. (How did he

get back?) By specially propelled parachute. (Where did it land?) In Africa. (Can we make something extraordinary happen here?) A strange kind of giraffe carried Mark and the soft brick to the Mediterranean. (Oh, I see Mark brought a pink brick with him. And next?) A subterranean creature with diamond false teeth took Mark and the brick to Greece – and then he went to Italy. (Now wait a minute. How did he get to Italy if he didn't have any money?) He sold the creature's diamond teeth to buy an air ticket – then over Europe by hovercraft – then under the English Channel, where Mark found the surface of the sea frozen over – so he put on propeller boots with metal studs and twisted himself like a drill till he reached the surface – then up the M1 in a modern car with wings which took off near Birmingham and brought him home . . . (What about the brick?) He found it tasted so nice – like strawberry ice cream – that he ate it.

This warming-up process, opening up doors into, and out of, the subconscious, and the oiling of the imagination laid the foundation for the morning's work. This was to make a composite, illustrated storybook.

Before we began I requested rough books at the ready and explained that as soon as they had 'invented' part of the story they were to write it down. Unless this was done they could forget their contribution. We then

brainstormed a theme: hat, elephant, rocket, cat and the class settled for a small box. Working in sequence, from child to child I navigated the story around the room.

The Snuff Box

Philip sat nearest the window so he began our story:

> 'A man is walking along with a snuff box in his pocket and he takes the snuff box, opens it, and puts some snuff in his nose, and he drops the snuff box and loses it in the grass.'

Seea continued:

> 'A midget comes along and finds the small box. He empties the snuff and puts some magic potion in it.'

The story then changed hands thirty more times; sometimes becoming repetitive, at other times stereotyped. Nevertheless it continued, held together by an ever-changing central focus. At moments where the lateral thinking seemed to be taking an obtuse direction I tried to steer it back again as unobtrusively as possible. This was particularly true as the story neared completion when I reminded the last four contributors that they had to bring the story to a close. A precis of the story would be something like this:

'A man drops a snuff box and loses it but it is found by a midget who replaces the snuff with a magic potion. Someone finds the potion and turns into a frog. A wizard's cat eats the frog and turns bright green. Then a spider eats the wizard. The spider which has become enormous falls down a grid in the road but climbs up again into a passing car. The family in the car visit an insectarium where the spider is declared a rare species. Growing gigantic again, the spider eventually reaches New York and climbs the Empire State Building. It falls off, demolishing buildings in the process, but the police eventually catch it and it turns back to its normal size. A man is walking along a path and he sees a small box . . .'

A rather unsynchronised story but standard for a first attempt.

The next stage was to distribute A4 paper and for pupils to draw a 2 cm margin down the left side on the horizontal format; this was to be the binding edge of the completed book when bound. The illustrated books shown earlier were produced again so the children could see how a storybook page can be designed; the text can be wrapped around illustrations; words and pictures balanced, often asymmetrically to produce a satisfying aesthetic unity. I drew some graphic layouts on the board showing approaches to page design: they had to ask themselves which part of their story sequence was most important and needed the most pronounced visual image on the page. If it were too small or poorly positioned it would fail to focus the attention of the eye; if it predominated too much it would fail to attract prolonged attention. The picture 'filled out' the story and revealed information the words could not provide. For example, the background scenario presented an environment which the words did not describe.

After the rough sketches which determined the relationship between text and illustrations, the class set to sketching out the page in light pencil. Horizontal lines indicated the placing of lines of words, and basic outlines suggested the placing of drawn objects. (Part of the brief was to include their names as part of the design.) From here they were free to continue as they wished. It was easier to fit the illustrations around the words than vice versa, so I suggested that the text should precede the artwork. One final point I made to the class was that I intended to photocopy the finished book so that strong linear work was preferable to light pencil work. The problem with this kind of suggestion is that children then think they have to put a thick black line around everything. They tend to do this at the best of times and my instructions were hardly designed to counteract the habit. I tried to help them to see how the main characteristics of a perceived object is rarely its outline but more likely what lies *inside* the form. I did two quick sketches on the board in an attempt to illustrate my point: one of a head and the other of a fireplace. Then I drew a thick black line round both pictures to show how it destroyed the logic of the free line image. All this was done in a few seconds and then rubbed off before anyone could start incorporating either image into their work. Teachers know that once an image, in any subject or media, is shown to a class it becomes instantaneously a model to be adopted. How one stimulates without indoctrinating children is one of the major concerns of teaching.

By this time we were half-way through the morning and so had just over an hour to develop the book page. The class worked quickly and I darted around the room checking the story line for mistakes before it was finally 'written in'. (In fact several children slipped through the net and there are some spelling and grammatical howlers in the collection.) The artwork developed at varying paces. The first person to say 'I've finished' was, if I agreed with him or her, commissioned to design the book cover. Often the pupils would declare that the work was completed but on inspection more could have been done to reap success. I don't think 'filling in' the empty spaces necessarily enhances or broadens a drawing's appeal. The converse is often true.

Philip's design (picture 1) contains only a schematic sun as background to the figure and tree and the strength to these images ensures

① A man is walking along with a snuff box in his pocket and he takes the snuff box, opens it, and puts some snuff in his nose, and he drops the snuff box and loses it in the grass.

Snuff box →

② A midget comes along and finds the snuff box. He empties the snuff and puts some magic potion in it.

③ Then a person came along and opened the Box and decided to try some of the magic potion

④ The person tried the potion and turned green and then in to a frog.

Claire Saville

⑤ The man who was turned into a frog dropped the box. Then a wizard came along and because he was a wizard he knew exactly what the potion was

RoGER BRTTISH

⑥ The Wizard came along and saw the cat with the frog in his throat and the cat turned bright green.

Vicky Lennon.

⑦ The Wizard turned really small. The cat put his tongue out and got the frog out.

⑧ And then the wizard could not turn back. Then a spider came along and ate the wizard up.

⑨ The Spider walks into the nearby city and was crushing everybody in his path.

⑩ One of the spiders legs got stuck in a grid and he couldnt get away.

HE WAS STUCK!

⑪ A car came along and went over the grid. The grid caved in and the spider fell down the grid.

⑫ The wizard climbs out of the window, falling onto the grass and leaving the spider in the car

13 Fred and his family go to the insectarium and the spider crawls onto his shoulder. They reach the insectarium and the attendant saw it and said it was a rare species.

INSECTARIUM

ENTRANCE

ADMISSION
CHILDREN £1
ADULTS £2
O.A.P'S £1

PAUL MITTEN

14 The spider gets put into a box, which used to belong to the dwarf and it has got a magic potion in it. And the spider grows to the size of Mount Everest.

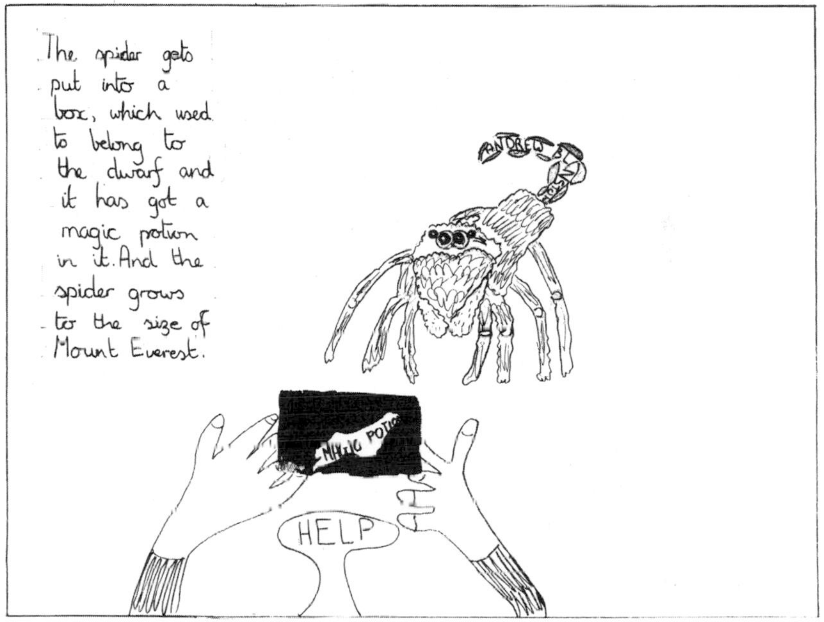

ANDREW

MAGIC POTION

HELP

15 The Spider got out of the box and went down a grill. He travled for thousands of miles and came up in New York and climbed up the Eempire State building

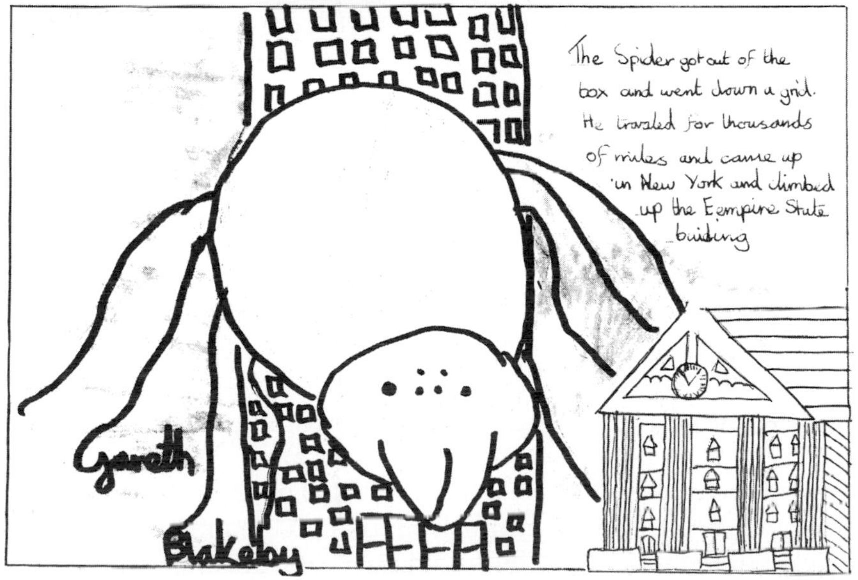

Gareth

Blakeby

16 About one hundred men came down the street carrying something very long and then one of the men said, "I think this leg belongs to you."

ANTHONY HOT

(17)

Meanwhile Fred is still trying to convince the police there's a Giant spider on the loose.

that it is in no sense an 'empty' composition. This is even more true of Magnus' layout (picture 17). The two figures are so consistently and confidently drawn in a graphic, sharp-edge style that anything else would have made the composition cluttered. We shall return to Magnus later, because with David (picture 12), it was clear that I had two budding graphic artists here. On one of my later teaching visits Magnus brought me his folder of drawings to show me. At ten he not only had a well-formed personal language of

drawing, but he could articulate verbally what he was doing and intending to do.

The artwork varies from the over-simple (picture 2) to the over-complex (pictue 11). Visual skills can lie several conceptual years apart. Iain (picture 8) draws everything without perspective from a front and side viewpoint. Whilst Mark (picture 9) makes a brave attempt at perspective and forshortening. Andrew (picture 14) became so engrossed in the spider drawing, concentrating on the minute detail of the facial

features that the rest of the page was ignored. Gareth (picture 15) conveys a very powerful central spider image, intensified by carefully drawn classical architecture.

There is probably greater consistency in verbal fluency than artwork but this is to be expected considering the emphasis on writing in the curriculum. What concerns me most here is not so much the indigenous standards of the verbal and visual material, but how they coexist on the picture plane.

The writing in picture 7 fits uncomfortably with the tree's branches, but Jannine (picture 3) makes a pleasing composition of juxtaposed words and images. In picture 2 both forms of communication stand well apart and unrelated but picture 17, whilst holding the two idioms apart, makes a visually satisfying composition. Perhaps Paul's (picture 13) is one of the most successful pieces. Here the words and clouds dance a polyphonic pattern and contrast with the solid building in the foreground. Vicky (pictue 6), still harnessed to the schematic sun and tree form, portrays the wizard and cat with a natural harmony. The total design holds the page well.

A week later I was able to deliver three bound copies of 'The Snuff Box' to Class 10, side-bound in yellow silk thread. No stimulus, however awe-inspiring, could have eclipsed the motivating effect that these books produced on the group. When I said 'For our next book . . .' I knew by the unremitting enthusiasm that greeted my words that these children, like me, were hooked on books.

Strictly speaking, I had deviated from the classical Japanese side-binding technique in binding 'The Snuff Box', for I had bound single, not folded leaves. The next project, however, was to make a more formal approach to the oriental art.

Side-bound story books

I had bought my first side-bound book only two years previously in a bookshop in Berkeley, California. It was P'u Ming's *Oxherding Pictures and Verses* translated from the classical Chinese by Red Pine. I showed this to the class, displaying how the writing and illustration lived in perfect harmony together; and later I took the book around the room (it was too delicate to be passed round) so they could see the beautifully textured rice paper from which the book was made.

Traditionally, Japanese four-hole binding is a style in which stitches are made at four points. Sometimes binding occurs in five holes (which is the Korean style) but in China, where preference for even numbers is culturally endemic, four-hole binding has been the order for centuries.

I explained to the class that in oriental binding the leaves are folded in half and then paginated separately (not one inside the other as in European bookbinding) with the fold on the outside, and the open ends of the folded sheet on the inside 'spine' of the book. There is no actual spinal strip to support the pages for, unlike Western books which place

tremendous tension down the centre spine, in oriental binding the tension is more evenly distributed *across* the spinal area. Another characteristic I wanted the children to observe was that the covers of my side-bound book were bound in the same manner as the pages inside and were, indeed, of much the same quality of paper (not thick paper as in Western paperbacks).

Perhaps the greatest advantage of the Japanese book is the organisational flexibility of its contents. With European bookbinding the number of pages to accommodate a 'one-off' story must be calculated before the final book writing can begin. The total number of words must be divided by the average number of words per book page; space for illustrations added to that; then pages added for title and end pages, before the number of pages required for the whole book can be drawn up and the writing begun. With side-binding no such elaborate planning is necessary. The formation of the book is simplicity itself; the pages following on one independently from the other, require nothing more than the author to construct the contents of the book in the same page-at-a-time manner. One simply adds pages as one goes along. If a page is spoilt in some way then it is replaced.

It was now time to embark on the pupil's own personal side-bound books, using the experience of group story making gained from the previous week's session. An A4 sheet of white paper had been divided into two A5

sections. The left section was ruled with lines, and the right left blank. About two hundred of these were duplicated, providing, I thought, enough leaves for everyone in the class. When folded, these sheets formed a writing right leaf and, on the reverse, a plain side for illustrations.

The class was then shown how a book of single sheets would be made. I produced a simulated book, completed with four-hole binding, and with this image of the book firmly planted in their minds I set to the story stimulation.

I brainstormed, not a theme, but the first few words of the story. Out of the many titles three were put to the vote:

1 In the middle of the night
2 It was lying there beside the path
3 As the water got higher

Number 2 won. I made a few suggestions: keep the story moving, introduce people, places and things when you feel the story needs it; aim for a climax of some kind and a resolution. I wanted them to imagine themselves as writers, writing and illustrating a book for children younger than themselves. This gave an added incentive for making the book and concentrated their minds on holding the interest of a reader. Stories were completed in draft and exchanged for 'proof-reading' (children are perhaps the most astute critics of literature!). The final version was started on the prepared paper. Pages were to be numbered centre bottom or top. (This avoided the possibility of numbering on the outer corners and thus losing the numbers in the binding.)

Children were at liberty to either write the story then illustrate, or to illustrate as they went along. It was a challenge to scan the written page and extract from it the essence of that part of the story for visual treatment. It is in tasks like this that the need to make a visual image energises the imagination. It is not simply illustrating a particular incident in a story, it is being faced with an unprecedented sequence of ideas which by accident of lines of writing come together as a page. It was from these chance relationships that a coherent picture image had to be composed. In the recorded interviews with children which follow, these kinds of problems, amongst others, are expressed.

A4 horizontal format – left A5 lined for written work, right A5 left blank for art/graphic work

'It was Yellow with Blue Spots' (*Catherine*)

Q What were you thinking about as you started the story?
A I wanted to make it interesting. I was trying to think about who might be reading the story.

'The Bowler Hat' (*Sarah*)

'My story is about a boy who finds a hat so he takes it home and in the morning he finds a man in it. The man says that to save the world he has to find a special flower hidden down a tunnel at the back of his garden. So the boy goes in search of it.'

Q Were there problems with matching the page of writing to an illustration?
A There wasn't always much happening that I could illustrate so I had to search in the story for something I could draw. I like reading science fiction and Agatha Christie. They gave me ideas of how to put a story together.

'The Buttermoth' (*Magnus*)

'I'd been doing some drawings and so I based my story on one of them. I decided I wanted it to be amusing and not serious. Some ideas came easily and some I had to think about a lot.

The story is about a monster who was found by the side of the road by another group of monsters. They wanted to brainwash it so that it would tell them where the really evil monster was.'

Q Did they succeed?
A No!
Q Drawing is something important to you, isn't it?
A Yes. I had the illustrations in my sketchbook at home and so I decided to use them for my story.
Q So you had to write the story to fit the illustrations?
A Yes, it was quite hard.
Q Do you think illustrations help you to 'see' a story better?
A Yes. For example, if a story is about a long dark classroom, like one of Roald Dahl's stories I can think of, the illustrator can include things in his picture which aren't in the story.
Q So the illustration 'fills in' some things which the story doesn't give you?
A Yes.

'The FBIZ' (*Gareth*)

'I like fantasy books and Roald Dahl's books and you can pick up tips from them to use when you write your own.

The story is about a boy who finds an aeroplane which he learns to fly but then, in the end, he has to give it back to the airforce.

In a good illustration you can imagine that you're inside the place illustrated. In the film '*Never Ending Story*', a boy reads a book and then imagines he's in the story. Sometimes with really good illustrations they can actually make you feel you're seeing the real thing.'

(*Catherine*)

'Sometimes I think it's good not to have illustrations so that you can invent the story in your own mind. But illustrations help you to see what's in an artist's mind. So if you are reading a story and then turn the page you can see if your idea is anything like that of the artist.'

(*Christine*)

'I like adventure stories.'

Q Does reading influence your writing?
A I think it helps with the wording and getting the expressions of people talking in your stories right.

'The Bowler Hat' (*David*)

'It's about a boy who finds an old bowler hat by the side of the road and he had to keep it from scientists who are trying to take it. It's a very valuable hat worn by King Henry in the seventeenth century. So the boy took it to the museum to keep it safe but a scientist there tries to steal it but it was safely looked after in the end.

I like watching cartoons on TV and then I try to draw them from memory.'

(*Paul*)

'I sometimes had difficulty in finding something on the page of writing I could draw, so in the end I took some small part of the story and illustrated that. It makes you use your imagination if you're stuck like that.'

By the fourth week the writing was completed and the illustrations matching each page of writing, drawn with pencil crayon and pen, were at the finishing stages. The penultimate process was designing the title page and making front and rear covers (it must be remembered that whereas Western bindings have one completed hinged cover, Eastern bindings have two independent covers). The inside fold of the outer covers became a decorative area, setting off the facing title page. In one case, where the book comprised several stories, a list of contents was placed on the reverse of the title page. The cover designs and title page were all afforded the same attention as the story and illustrations. I made sketches on the board suggesting ways in which cover title, author and artwork could be juxtaposed into an integrated design. We looked at different kinds of letterface designs and discussed the appropriateness of letter design to story content. A ghostly story might require different letter shapes to a science fiction story set on Mars. Similarly, the cover artwork had not only to reflect the story behind it but attract the eye to it. I knew that much more time was needed on these important book art aspects than I had allowed. My dilemma was whether to prolong the project and give detailed attention to design, or to terminate the production at this level of understanding. I chose the latter because, relying on instinct, I felt that the book concept had been taken as far as was appropriate at that time. The attention it deserved would accumulate over a period of time.

The final process was pagination – ensuring the pages were in the right order – and then binding, using bulldog clips or the home-made presses to secure the loose pages before stitching. I demonstrated the authentic Japanese four-hole binding technique but I gave the class freedom to determine the number and arrangement of binding holes as they wished. I thought it would personalise the process if pupils made their own pattern of holes thus creating a hall-mark signature of their own. Distances between holes were measured and most children found little difficulty in using the awl to make holes through the layers of paper before the stitching. The stitching, though, proved harder, for, whilst European binding follows a simple over-under pattern, side-binding can be more complex, especially if an elaborate pattern is sewn. However, although a fixed sewing pattern can be imposed, almost any route can be taken, for one is sure to finish up eventually where one started and tie a knot! Perhaps the free spirit within me prefers this course of non-specific action, because, as an incurable empiricist, I believe that trial and error is by far the best educator.

Some children, as might be expected, were

Japanese side (four-hold) binding

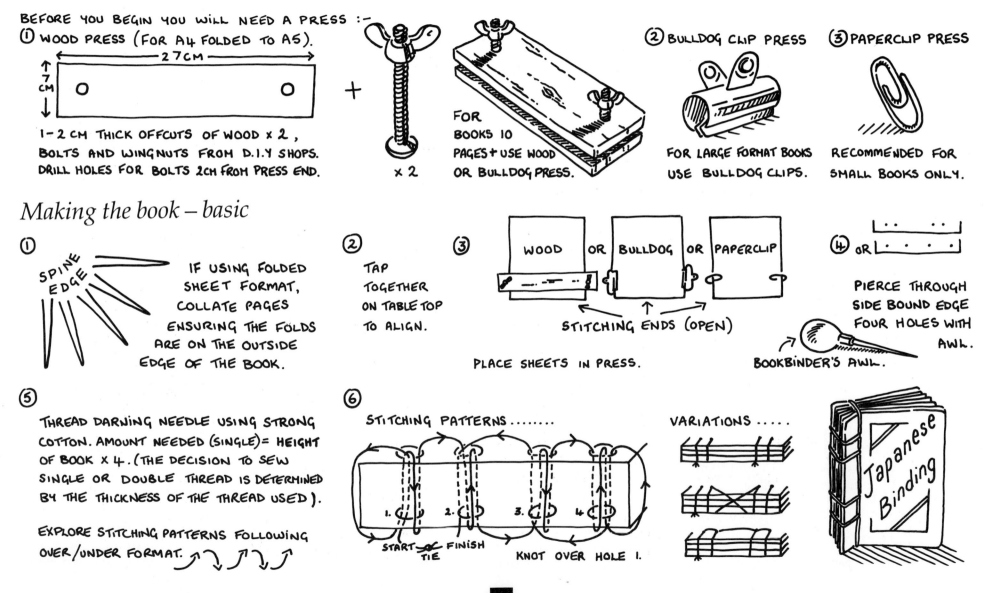

BEFORE YOU BEGIN YOU WILL NEED A PRESS :-
① WOOD PRESS (FOR A4 FOLDED TO A5).

← 27CM →

↑ 7 CM ↓

1-2 CM THICK OFFCUTS OF WOOD × 2,
BOLTS AND WINGNUTS FROM D.I.Y SHOPS.
DRILL HOLES FOR BOLTS 2CM FROM PRESS END.

× 2

FOR
BOOKS 10
PAGES + USE WOOD
OR BULLDOG PRESS.

② BULLDOG CLIP PRESS

FOR LARGE FORMAT BOOKS
USE BULLDOG CLIPS.

③ PAPERCLIP PRESS

RECOMMENDED FOR
SMALL BOOKS ONLY.

Making the book – basic

① SPINE EDGE

IF USING FOLDED
SHEET FORMAT,
COLLATE PAGES
ENSURING THE FOLDS
ARE ON THE OUTSIDE
EDGE OF THE BOOK.

② TAP
TOGETHER
ON TABLE TOP
TO ALIGN.

③ WOOD OR BULLDOG OR PAPERCLIP

STITCHING ENDS (OPEN)

PLACE SHEETS IN PRESS.

④ OR

PIERCE THROUGH
SIDE BOUND EDGE
FOUR HOLES WITH
AWL.

BOOKBINDER'S AWL.

⑤ THREAD DARNING NEEDLE USING STRONG
COTTON. AMOUNT NEEDED (SINGLE) = HEIGHT
OF BOOK × 4. (THE DECISION TO SEW
SINGLE OR DOUBLE THREAD IS DETERMINED
BY THE THICKNESS OF THE THREAD USED).

EXPLORE STITCHING PATTERNS FOLLOWING
OVER/UNDER FORMAT.

⑥ STITCHING PATTERNS........

1. 2. 3. 4.

START TIE FINISH

KNOT OVER HOLE 1.

VARIATIONS .....

Japanese Binding

Japanese side binding – hard cover

1 Open (4 section)

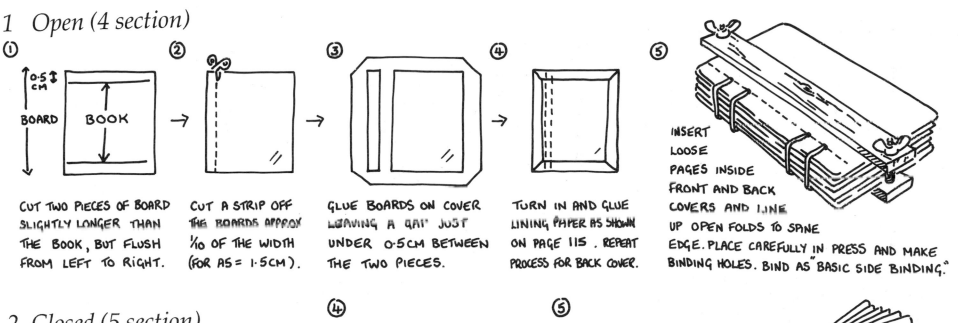

① 0·5 CM / BOARD / BOOK

CUT TWO PIECES OF BOARD SLIGHTLY LONGER THAN THE BOOK, BUT FLUSH FROM LEFT TO RIGHT.

② CUT A STRIP OFF THE BOARDS APPROX 1/10 OF THE WIDTH (FOR A5 = 1·5 CM).

③ GLUE BOARDS ON COVER LEAVING A GAP JUST UNDER 0·5CM BETWEEN THE TWO PIECES.

④ TURN IN AND GLUE LINING PAPER AS SHOWN ON PAGE 115. REPEAT PROCESS FOR BACK COVER.

⑤ INSERT LOOSE PAGES INSIDE FRONT AND BACK COVERS AND LINE UP OPEN FOLDS TO SPINE EDGE. PLACE CAREFULLY IN PRESS AND MAKE BINDING HOLES. BIND AS "BASIC SIDE BINDING."

2 Closed (5 section)

THIS PROCESS IS SIMILAR TO THE ABOVE METHOD EXCEPT A SPINE IS ADDED AND THE BOOK IS THEREFORE CLOSED AT THE SPINE.

FOLLOW THE ABOVE PROCEDURE FOR STAGES ① + ② THEN ADD ANOTHER STRIP THE SAME LENGTH AS THE OTHER TWO PIECES ③. THE SPINE'S WIDTH IS DETERMINED BY THE NUMBER OF PAGES IN THE BOOK WHICH SHOULD BE APPROXIMATELY THE WIDTH OF THE BOOKS PAGES × 2.

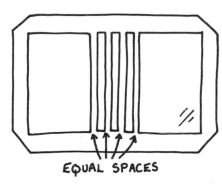

④ EQUAL SPACES

ATTACH BOARDS AND LEAVE SAME SPACES AS "OPEN BINDING" ABOVE.

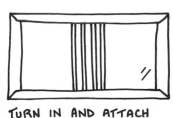

⑤ TURN IN AND ATTACH LINING AS ABOVE.

⑥ FOLD COVER UP AND INSERT BOOK. BIND AS ABOVE.

POEMS OF FUJI

Japanese side binding

3 Three section cover book

Hard cover book

THIS METHOD IS VERY ADAPTABLE TO LARGE SCALE WORK. THE DESIGN HERE IS FOR A4 FORMAT SINGLE HORIZONTAL SHEET (UNFOLDED.)

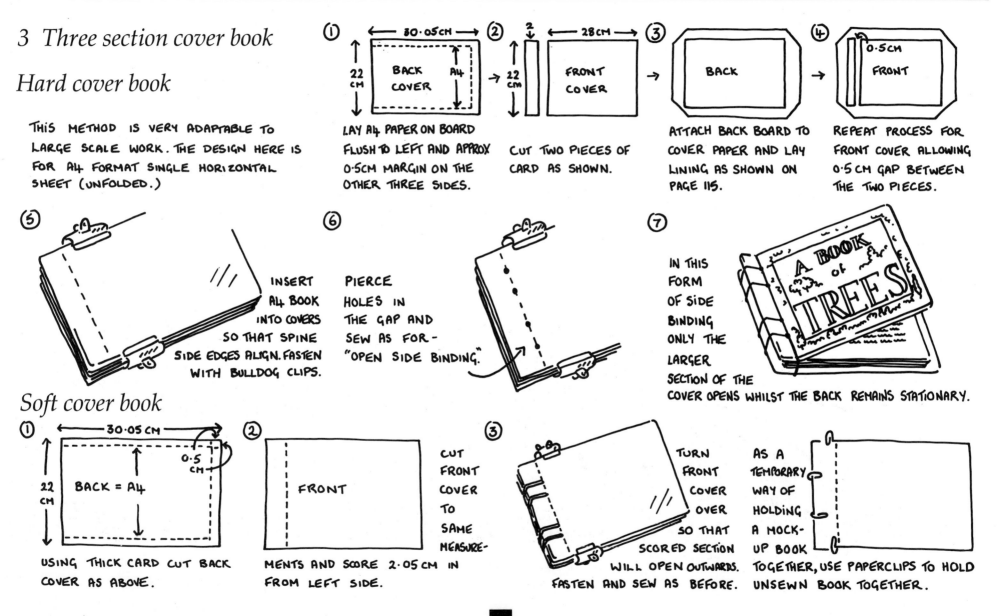

① LAY A4 PAPER ON BOARD FLUSH TO LEFT AND APPROX 0·5CM MARGIN ON THE OTHER THREE SIDES.

30·05CM · 22 CM · BACK COVER · A4

② CUT TWO PIECES OF CARD AS SHOWN.

2 · 22 CM · 28CM · FRONT COVER

③ ATTACH BACK BOARD TO COVER PAPER AND LAY LINING AS SHOWN ON PAGE 115.

BACK

④ REPEAT PROCESS FOR FRONT COVER ALLOWING 0·5 CM GAP BETWEEN THE TWO PIECES.

0·5CM · FRONT

⑤ INSERT A4 BOOK INTO COVERS SO THAT SPINE SIDE EDGES ALIGN. FASTEN WITH BULLDOG CLIPS.

⑥ PIERCE HOLES IN THE GAP AND SEW AS FOR "OPEN SIDE BINDING."

⑦ IN THIS FORM OF SIDE BINDING ONLY THE LARGER SECTION OF THE COVER OPENS WHILST THE BACK REMAINS STATIONARY.

A BOOK of TREES

Soft cover book

① USING THICK CARD CUT BACK COVER AS ABOVE.

30·05 CM · 22 CM · BACK = A4 · 0.5 CM

② CUT FRONT COVER TO SAME MEASUREMENTS AND SCORE 2·05 CM IN FROM LEFT SIDE.

FRONT

③ TURN FRONT COVER OVER SO THAT SCORED SECTION WILL OPEN OUTWARDS. FASTEN AND SEW AS BEFORE.

AS A TEMPORARY WAY OF HOLDING A MOCK-UP BOOK TOGETHER, USE PAPERCLIPS TO HOLD UNSEWN BOOK TOGETHER.

handier than others at sewing. Some produced intricate woven patterns of near embroidery, and others found even single hole tying almost an impossibility. Using double thread produced its own problems (as always) especially when 'pulling through' the thread, a process which tends to create a little bundle of knots. The way to avoid this it to pull through the thread slowly, checking for the formation of knots or, ideally, for a partner to hold the thread taut as it is pulled through. Knot tying itself, of course, created problems but working in pairs, each borrowing the other's finger, when required, helped.

The sewing was by far the most exasperating part of the whole book production. Several children made many attempts at getting the sewing right, and I tuned my ears to detect noises of despair which, decoded, said 'Help!' Fortunately, not more than four or five children finished the pagination at the same time so there was no rush on the limited presses, clips, awls and needles at my disposal.

I should add that before the final binding took place all the books were photocopied in their loose, open A4 format and then bound as the originals. In this way, whoever retained the original, other interested parties like myself could have a copy. It is worth emphasising here that black ink gives a much sharper reproduction than dark blue – a point worth remembering if photocopying books is envisaged.

The side-binding project had taken four to five mornings to complete (although David was still working on his book three weeks after everyone else had finished theirs). Most children had shown themselves capable of putting a story together. The shortest book comprised three pages of writing; the largest eight; the average five. The longest stories were not necessarily the best and many lacked a well-shaped plot, with an inclination to 'jump' from one situation to another without 'stepping stones' and for endings to be sudden and unresolved. Illustrations varied too, and were conceptually weaker than the writing. Pupils easily fell back on stereotyped images gleaned from popular sources. The decorative elements of the cover designs, more a preoccupation at the expense of design, probably came from pattern work in

Carefully folding pages from A4 to A5

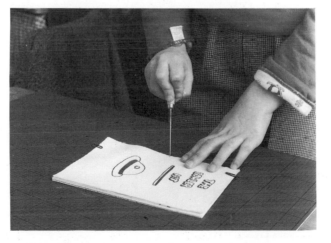

Using bookbinder's awl to pierce holes for four-hole binding (paperclip press)

Stitching four-hole side binding

earlier years. But I was generally satisfied with the results. It was, after all, their first ever self-made book and their enthusiasm and commitment had been enlightening.

In all the book art production done so far with children, I had not employed the European central binding technique using hard covers. Whether or not this was an oversight I am uncertain; somehow the need for it hadn't really arisen. I have already said that traditional bookbinding in the classroom can be deadly, and perhaps it was for this reason that, unconsciously, I had sidetracked it for alternative routes to book art.

Somewhere, from a voice within, came the call to spend my last major project with children exploring European hard cover binding, or rather an adaption of it to suit the needs of children.

Magnus decided to break with tradition and stitch a three-hole pattern

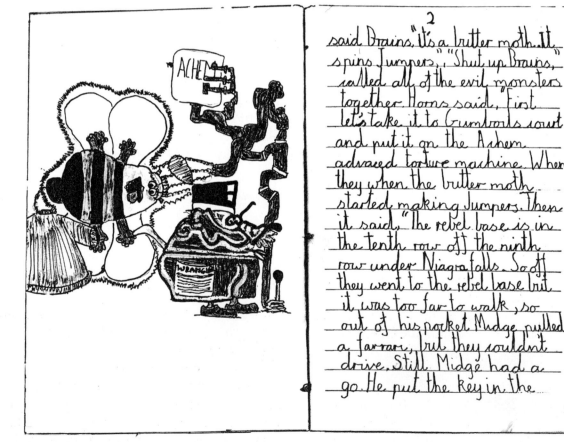

Books with hard covers

This next activity was carried out with the sixth year of Brookburn Primary School. The strategy was for pupils to work in pairs. This provides a number of advantages: shared ideas in story writing often produce surprising and unexpected solutions to plot development. As in conversation, a wholly original way of looking at a situation can be experienced. Our imagination is as much a prison as a source of revelation. A 'lost' or 'stuck' story can be revitalised by the involvement of another author. Another advantage of shared working is that the process, from conception to completion, is quickened. There is less likelihood that the story will lose its impetus, specially towards the end. Also, pupils' strengths can be utilised to the full; tasks delegated to match preferences and aptitudes, for example writing, illustration, design, lettering. But essentially it is the social element which is so important here. The skills of working as a team, organising a working structure and solving problems jointly as they arrive. The class was arranged into friendship pairs and a group improvisation set in motion.

It was agreed that the book would comprise ten pages arranged on six A5 leaves folded from three A4 sheets of cartridge paper (plus an endpaper page). Several book simulations and blackboard graphics illustrated the chronological sequence of endpaper (later to be glued to the cover), title pages, text and

Group improvisation

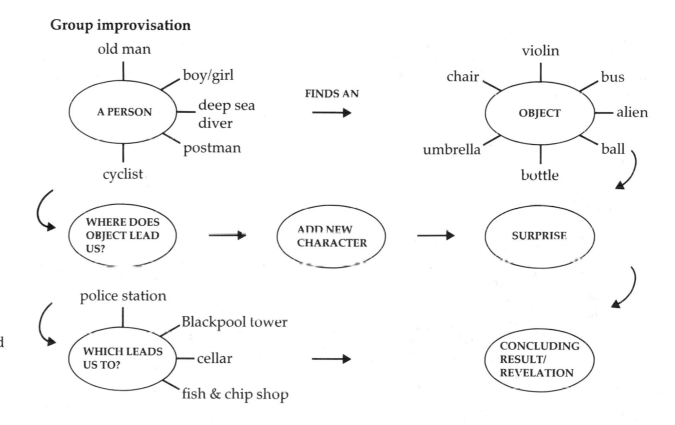

illustrations. Writing was designated to left side pages (1, 3, 5, 7, 9) and illustrations to right side pages (2, 4, 6, 8, 10).

The usefulness of these blackboard graphics was to suggest the number of sentences appropriate to the story form, for example if a page was half writing and half blank space, this would imply, say, three sentences. Using this technique, the whole story could be allocated to the five writing pages even before the writing of the first draft had begun. Writing a story to fit a book, rather than the more usual way of fitting a book around a story, is a technique I discussed earlier. I so often observe children writing stories in book form without any real concept of the book itself. This can result in an unsatisfactory presentation, like, for example, words being

Book pages

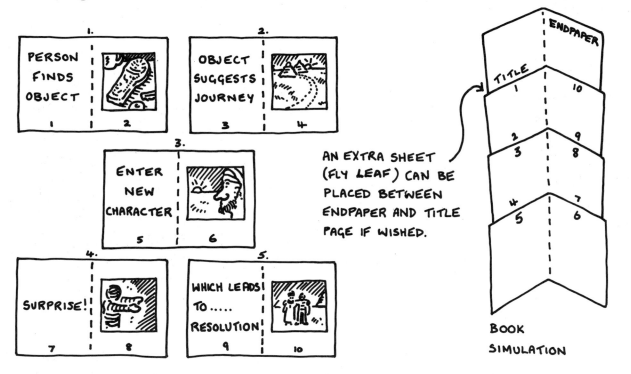

1.

PERSON FINDS OBJECT	
1	2

2.

OBJECT SUGGESTS JOURNEY	
3	4

3.

ENTER NEW CHARACTER	
5	6

4.

SURPRISE!	
7	8

5.

WHICH LEADS TO..... RESOLUTION	
9	10

AN EXTRA SHEET (FLY LEAF) CAN BE PLACED BETWEEN ENDPAPER AND TITLE PAGE IF WISHED.

ENDPAPER

TITLE

1	10
2	9
3	8
4	7
5	6

BOOK SIMULATION

progress unhindered. The corrected rough drafts were exchanged, read, criticised and final presentation applied to fit the A5 format.

Jack produced some of the most satisfying illustrations. The centre page drawing of Jack's part of the story includes a careful study of his own left hand. Suzanne's centre page spread is a successful arrangement of shapes, textures and text. The path logically carried the eye across the page.

As the books were completed, a title page design was produced for the reverse side of page one, and finally a blank sheet of A4 wrapped around the completed storybook. (This would later be glued down to the cover boards.)

My original aim had been for the pupils to cut their own cover boards, but with ever-decreasing time available for the project, I did this myself. Medium weight cartridge paper was cut to a dimension approximately 2 cm larger than the cover board and spine dimensions. This became the book cover. Diagrams went on the board showing how the cover design would fit on to the book when finished. It was still difficult for many pupils to conceive the flat sheet of paper as a three-dimensional book cover. An important factor was that the parameter of the cover, a 2 cm margin, would eventually be folded over and glued down to the inside cover boards. This was not clearly understood by some pupils, placing titles too high, and then finding the tops of letters disappearing over the top edge of the cover boards.

squeezed together because the page space is inadequate. The European bound book is a special problem because unlike concertina and side-bound books, the structure is from the centre outwards. Careful planning is necessary if a book of too many or too few pages is to be avoided.

From this beginning, the pair-drafting began. If pupil 'A' was responsible for writing, pupil 'B' would draft artwork, whilst both being responsible for the story. When an episode was too long to fit on the page, aesthetically, the pair set about extracting the essence of it and reduced it accordingly.

If too few words were forthcoming, either discussion was required to enlarge the plot or artwork/design incorporated instead. As only one of the pair could work on the book page at any one time, it was decided to present finished writing on separate paper to be pasted into the book on completion. This enabled the illustration of the book to

Page from 'The Return of the Bottle' by Ben and Jack (11)

Page from 'The Drawing Pin' by Suzanne and Carolyn (11)

The next stage was the stitching. I demonstrated a conventional five hole over/under stitching pattern. One of the advantages of pupils working at varying speeds is that the demand on tools and equipment like darning needles can be eased. As groups of four to six children finished the presentation I could show them the stitching technique again, this time at close quarters and give advice individually.

The cover design had to take into account front and back covers, spine and fold-over margins. It was possible, however, for the spinal title to be done after the final assembly,

and some pupils did this, although it does require very dexterous penmanship. I showed the class professionally designed book covers so they could see:

1 how the essence of the story contained within the book is expressed in the cover design;
2 that through colour and the arrangement of shapes the eye is attracted to the book by its cover;
3 that the words are an integral part of the design; and
4 that lettering is an art form.

Both book artists, I thought, should work on the cover design, and although this was a relatively small area, this did not prove too great a difficulty. Artwork tended to be shared, but some pairs like Ben and Jack decided to delegate artwork and lettering as separate tasks.

The next stage was the placing of the cover boards on the reverse side of the cover design. Traditionally, children have been required to paste down the whole of the cover paper to the boards. I have never done this with any of my own books, or found it necessary. In fact I find the less adhesive used the better. It is my practice to use a tiny dot of adhesive on the centre of the cover boards and spine, and this just holds it in place on the cover paper. Providing the turned-in cover is securely attached, the book is as secure as any other method of book binding. This is the procedure I used with the children. Next the corner mitres are cut, the turned-in flaps brushed along the edges with latex adhesive and pressed firmly down to the cover boards. This was demonstrated to small groups as they neared this stage of the production. I cut a mitre from one of the corners of the cover paper freehand, using my eye to judge the 45° angle. I wondered if I could expect this of the children (and indeed if they should use knives at all) but as they were closely supervised I took the risk and was delighted with the result. They did some test runs first, practising eye-measured 45° angles on odd paper fragments until they felt able to attend to the cover mitres. They did this accurately and cleanly, with the precision of a surgeon, remembering to leave a gap the thickness of the cover board at the corner. (With thin cover paper it is possible to avoid cutting mitres and to simply fold the corners into the boards; however, with heavier paper, like the cartridge we were using, this method would have produced an unpleasant bulge at the corners, so was best avoided.)

It is for the class teacher, with his/her knowledge of the individual pupils, to decide what the teacher does, and what can be reasonably expected of the children. The

The cover design after binding. The original design was 2 cm larger than the cover boards to allow for 'turning-in'

'The Drawing Pin' by Suzanne and Carolyn

mitres can be cut with scissors, but as the paper is best left flat, cutting with a knife on a cutting mat is preferable.

Here again, I must confess to not keeping to the traditional roles of book binding. The process I have described so far is largely a 'rule of eye' method because this is the way I make my own books. I 'measure' hardly anything – using my eye to sense accuracy. If the cover boards, the spine, the gaps between them, and the thickness of the boards were all mechanically measured then the exact size of the cover paper could be calculated and the cover cut to size. The mitres could then be cut using scissors in a normally held position. Some teachers may wish to do this and indeed

see it as a mathematical skill exercise. I fully endorse this approach but it is not the way I wish to work with children. I have developed a very keen eye and try to evolve the same skills in those I teach. It is after all the oldest skill of all, an innate skill known to every African tribesman but largely lost to our own society which relies for nearly everything on mechanical devices.

As each pair of book artists came to me ready for the joining of the book to its cover I adopted the following procedure: I turned in the top, longer fold and glued it over the head, as I have already said by running the brush swiftly along the edge. There is no need to completely cover this strip; a well attached

European binding (basic)

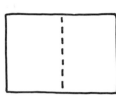

FOLD BOOK PAGES
IN HALF. THE END
PAGE WILL EVENTUALLY BE GLUED DOWN
TO COVERS SO LEAVE BLANK.

SUPERIMPOSE PAGES
TO FORM BOOK.

HOLD OPEN BOOK STEADY
(OR FASTEN WITH CLIPS) AND
PIERCE HOLES DOWN SPINE.

TOP + BOTTOM HOLES 1CM FROM EDGE.

OR · OR

EXPLORE HOLE PATTERNS.
HOLES NO MORE THAN
5CM APART.

BEGIN
END · TIE

SEW
AND TIE
FROM BACK OF BOOK.

Hard cover

① WITH THE BOOK CLOSED LAY ON BOARD AND
ALLOW 0.5CM TOP AND BOTTOM BUT FLUSH
TO LEFT AND RIGHT. CUT BOARD COVERS (x2)
AND SPINE. SPINE WIDTH = 3/4 X CLOSED
(UNBOUND) BOOK. THE MORE PAGES THE
BOOK HAS, THE WIDER THE SPINE. 1CM IS
ADEQUATE FOR 10-15 PAGES.

BOOK

② ← CUT MITRES →

ALLOW 2 MATCHSTICK WIDTHS
BETWEEN COVERS + SPINE.

③ ATTACH COVER TO BOARDS
AND LINING TO INSIDE
COVER AS SHOWN ON PAGE 115.

④ BACK OF STITCHED BOOK

APPLY ADHESIVE TO CENTRE
SPINE AND LIGHTLY TO
BORDER EDGES ON ONE SIDE.

⑤ BOOK COVER

BOOK

ALIGN BOOK OVER COVER
AND LAY CENTRALLY.
APPLY LIGHT PRESSURE TO
SPINE IN OUTWARDS DIRECTION.

⑥

LIFT
BACK AND APPLY
ADHESIVE TO EDGES.

⑦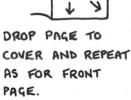

DROP PAGE TO
COVER AND REPEAT
AS FOR FRONT
PAGE.

⑧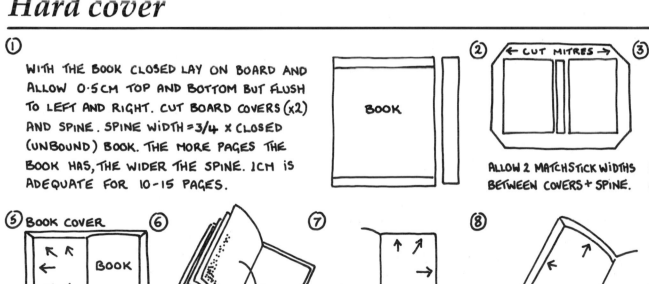

OPEN BOOK
TO FRONT
PAGE AND GENTLY FINGER
SCORE SPINE + EDGES.

AGAIN , AS YOU RAISE
FRONT COVER. REPEAT
TO BACK OF BOOK.

LEAVE
FOR A
FEW MINUTES
THEN FINGER
SCORE SPINE

MY
BOOK

GENTLY
FINGER SCORE SPINE
EDGES INTO GROVE.

European binding

Soft cover

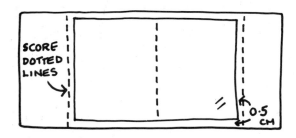

FOLLOW BASIC BINDING TO STITCHING STAGE THEN LAY BOOK ON CARTRIDGE SHEET. ALLOW 0.5CM MARGIN TOP AND BOTTOM AND ENOUGH MARGIN LEFT AND RIGHT TO FOLD IN AS COVER FLAPS.

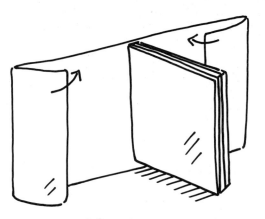

STITCH AS FOR BASIC BOOK BUT START ON INSIDE AND THUS TIE KNOT INSIDE OF SPINE.

Card cover

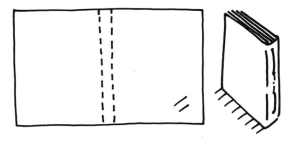

BASICALLY THE SAME TECHNIQUE CAN BE APPLIED TO A CARD COVER. SCORE SPINE X 2 WIDTHS OF BOOK + FOLLOW PROCEDURE FOR SOFT COVER BOOK.

Additions to bound books

FOLDING PAGE WITH PAPER CLASP.

PAGE WITH FLAPS.

PAGE WITH POCKETS

CONCERTINA BOOK BOUND INTO CENTRALLY BOUND BOOK.

MULTI-FORMED BOOK.

OPENING OUT MAP OR DIAGRAM.

edge will give the book all the strength it needs. Latex adhesive, remember, has a working life of only a few seconds – its bain and its blessing – so this running of the brush along the edge must be as light and swift as a ballet dancer's movement. Always use minimum adhesive (don't feel you must apply it thickly because if you do, it will all flood out when you 'press down' and give you the unnecessary task of peeling it all off later). I then gently but firmly press the strip down to the cover boards from the head-edge inwards (to press or apply pressure in any other direction will amost certainly create creases). It is important to run one's finger and apply pressure along the point at which the paper crosses the edge of the board as one attaches the flap down. If this is not done a gap usually appears between board and cover which is untidy in appearance. One of the pair then proceeded to turn in the shorter, left fold and fastened it over the fore-edge following my example. The remaining pupil did the same to the right fold and then one of us completed the turning-in by glueing the bottom fold over the tail. If these folds are not satisfactorily completed they can carefully be peeled free again, providing only a short time has elapsed since glueing. The old latex can be peeled off, a new layer applied and the turning-in tried a second (and hopefully final) time.

Finally, in this seemingly complex set of procedures comes the attaching of the single section book to the completed cover. This

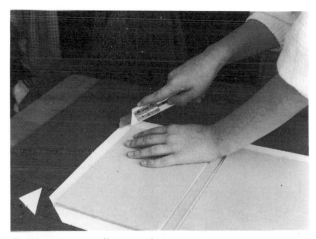
Cutting corner mitres on the cover

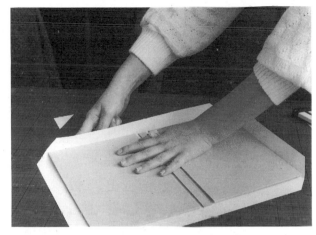
Cover edge 'finger scored' over cover boards

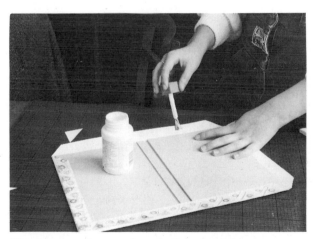
Glueing down to cover boards (turning in)

Glueing book pages into cover

should be the simplest task of all and would be if latex adhesive didn't dry so quickly! My own method, with all but the smallest books, is to apply the adhesive to the spine of the book first and then to run the brush smoothly (and quickly) along the three edges of the left endpaper; align the book vertically and horizontally to cover and then lower book to cover; open to centre page and press firmly down to spine; open quickly to left endpaper and run fingers down the spine and then outwards/upwards to head of endpaper, outwards/downwards to tail, and outwards across to the fore-edge. When pressing down the endpapers always spread in an outwards direction. Now it is the turn of the right side of the book which should be processed in the same way. Lining up the book to the cover can be difficult. First-attempt books are sometimes spoilt because the pages are 'out of true' with the cover. If this happens, all is not lost if you act quickly. Gently peel away the endpaper from the cover, and, providing the latex has not yet coagulated, it is still possible to reset. However, if the latex is already setting, which is probably the case, let it solidify and then peel it off in a film. If the endpaper is of reasonably heavy paper, and the peeling off process has not torn or damaged it, it may be possible to re-latex and try the marrying of book to cover again. Whenever this infuriating situation happens to me I usually cut out the stitching, replace the endpaper, restitch and re-latex again with my fingers crossed! With these children I glued the spine

and left endpaper, placed the book on the cover but let the pupils press down the spine and endpaper. They then repeated this on the other side of the book but this time they were responsible for both glueing and pressing down.

The completed book was then left to set for a few minutes. All that remains to be done at this stage is for the front cover to be raised carefully to the vertical position. As this is done the index finger of the right hand should gently score the spine edge of the endpaper. This prevents the endpaper bubbling up under the pressure of being raised. The same should be done to the back cover. On the outside of the book gently indent (with the finger tip) the cover paper into the spinal grooves. This gives a pleasing raised effect to the spine. Needless to say the hand should be clean for these final stages. Any surplus latex adhesive to be found can be carefully 'rolled off' when set. (I think it only fair to repeat that much of what I have suggested runs contrary to traditional school book binding practice; it is very much a 'personal view' not an orthodox methodology.)

As one by one the books were finished, the room vibrated with a wonderful sense of accomplishment. Yet still a critical eye prevailed. Discrepancies previously concealed in the 'becoming' process now became noticeable. Cover designs conceived in the flat looked different when folded so extra artwork was sometimes applied. Title pages were less convincing than at first thought, endpapers

and fly leaves looked in need of some kind of decoration.

The books were passed around the room to be viewed, read and 'experienced', for the books were objects of aesthetic meaning independent of what they contained. When a few days later they were covered in acetate film to protect them, the books on display aroused more interest than all the school library books put together.

It had been yet another crash programme. My most ambitious book project achieved in four to five afternoons. Not surprisingly, all manner of imperfections are evident in them from story, grammar, handwriting to cover design and binding. But to have entered this hard cover book project at a deeper, more prolonged level of expectation would not have been a success. Had I been able to work with them all week, over a longer period of time, and had it not been the summer term, increasingly reaching its far end, my tactics would have been different. But the advantage of this truncated project was that it provided evidence that a book, and a well-made book at that, complete in every way with story and illustrations can be made by children (with some assistance) in a very limited and fragmented period of time.

 Other types of books

Computerised books

No book artist is complete without informational technology skills. The access to writing that computerised story making makes available is essential to language development far beyond the immediate confines of this book. Here are just three examples of word-processed books.

'The Adventures of Furry the Gerbil' by Christopher and Daniel (infants). This comprises five pages of print supported by artwork. The computer printout has been attached to lightweight cartridge holding the artwork on the reverse side. An extended left-hand margin has enabled binding by the side-bound method.

'Our Minibeast Hunt' is a collection of poems written (and word-processed) in pairs by middle juniors. The poems are beautifully mounted with illustrations, and the whole is bound as a concertina book in hard covers.

'3C Strikes Again' by Emma (top junior) is an arrangement of computer processed text and illustration. The book was designed around the printout material, centrally bound, and then text and illustration pasted into the pages.

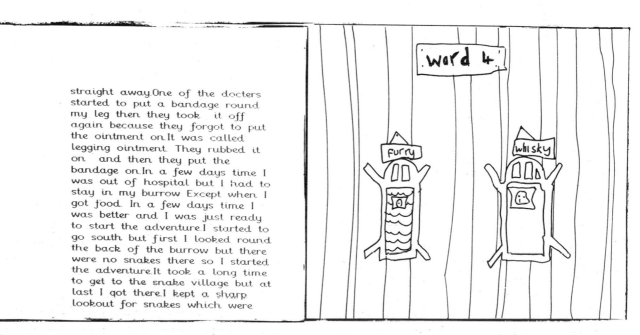

straight away. One of the docters started to put a bandage round my leg then they took it off again because they forgot to put the ointment on. It was called legging ointment. They rubbed it on and then they put the bandage on. In a few days time I was out of hospital but I had to stay in my burrow Except when I got food. In a few days time I was better and I was just ready to start the adventure. I started to go south but first I looked round the back of the burrow but there were no snakes there so I started the adventure. It took a long time to get to the snake village but at last I got there. I kept a sharp lookout for snakes which were

'The Adventures of Furry the Gerbil' by Christopher and Daniel

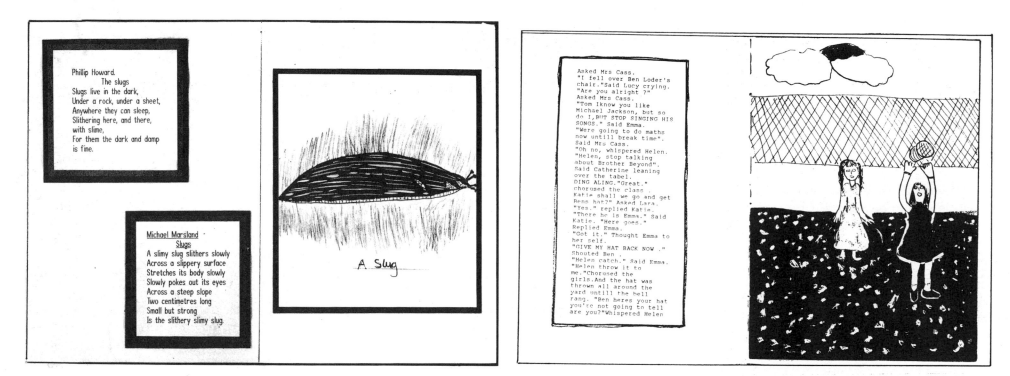

'Our Minibeast Hunt'

'3C Strikes Again'

Theme books

Theme books enable a class topic to be bound together. Not only are they hugely popular with children, they can become useful resource material in the classroom, decorate wall spaces if hung, and provide an effective protection of children's work to be stored.

   All the binding methods already discussed can be employed, although there is a tendency for books to be of a larger format than individual books.

'Feel' book (side-bound) (Nursery)

Large format side-bound theme book. Black sugar paper was folded in half to make pages and the complete book stitched with wool (Infants)

The pages of this A1 size book were joined together by a paper strip and the ends bound as an 'open' concertina book using paper covered boards (Infants)

In this theme book each child in the class was given a letter of the alphabet to draw using words beginning with the appropriate letter as the source of visual imagery e.g. 'O' = Octopus, 'P' = Plant (Year four – side-bound on unfolded A1 sheets)

*'The Tree' – Poems and observational drawings
(Year three)*

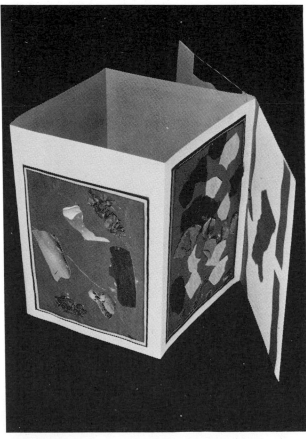 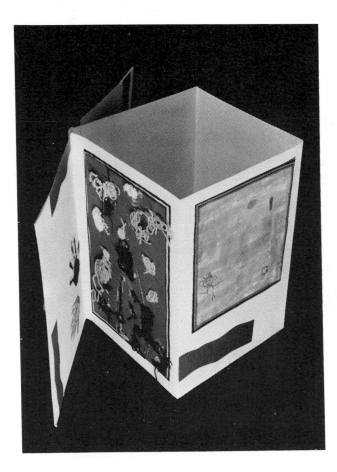

3D Theme book on the colour blue (Nursery)

Appendix 1 – General hints on making books

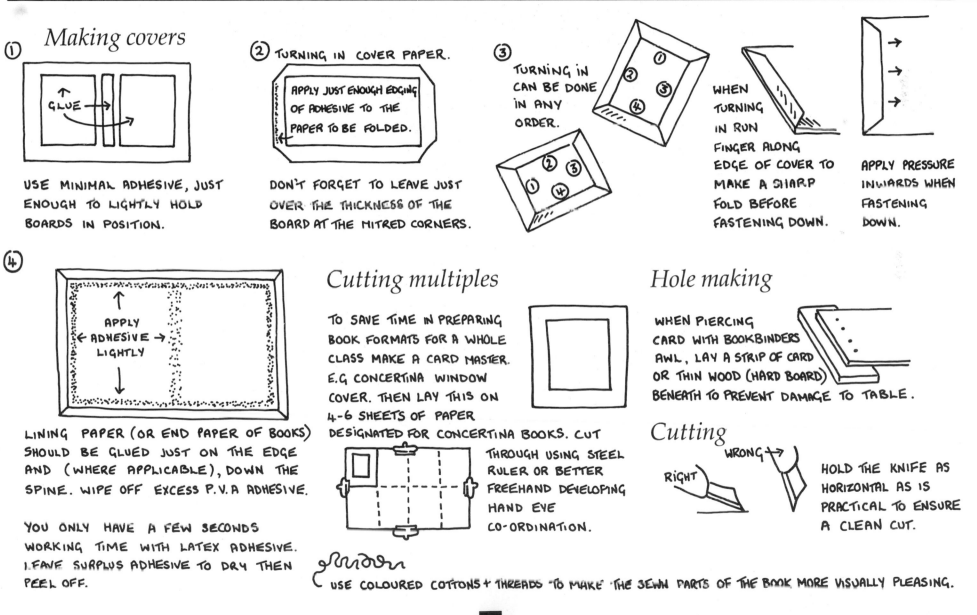

① Making covers

GLUE

USE MINIMAL ADHESIVE, JUST ENOUGH TO LIGHTLY HOLD BOARDS IN POSITION.

② TURNING IN COVER PAPER.

APPLY JUST ENOUGH EDGING OF ADHESIVE TO THE PAPER TO BE FOLDED.

DON'T FORGET TO LEAVE JUST OVER THE THICKNESS OF THE BOARD AT THE MITRED CORNERS.

③ TURNING IN CAN BE DONE IN ANY ORDER.

WHEN TURNING IN RUN FINGER ALONG EDGE OF COVER TO MAKE A SHARP FOLD BEFORE FASTENING DOWN.

APPLY PRESSURE INWARDS WHEN FASTENING DOWN.

④

APPLY ADHESIVE LIGHTLY

LINING PAPER (OR END PAPER OF BOOKS) SHOULD BE GLUED JUST ON THE EDGE AND (WHERE APPLICABLE), DOWN THE SPINE. WIPE OFF EXCESS P.V.A ADHESIVE.

YOU ONLY HAVE A FEW SECONDS WORKING TIME WITH LATEX ADHESIVE. LEAVE SURPLUS ADHESIVE TO DRY THEN PEEL OFF.

Cutting multiples

TO SAVE TIME IN PREPARING BOOK FORMATS FOR A WHOLE CLASS MAKE A CARD MASTER. E.G CONCERTINA WINDOW COVER. THEN LAY THIS ON 4-6 SHEETS OF PAPER DESIGNATED FOR CONCERTINA BOOKS. CUT THROUGH USING STEEL RULER OR BETTER FREEHAND DEVELOPING HAND EYE CO-ORDINATION.

USE COLOURED COTTONS + THREADS TO MAKE THE SEWN PARTS OF THE BOOK MORE VISUALLY PLEASING.

Hole making

WHEN PIERCING CARD WITH BOOKBINDERS AWL, LAY A STRIP OF CARD OR THIN WOOD (HARD BOARD) BENEATH TO PREVENT DAMAGE TO TABLE.

Cutting

WRONG

RIGHT

HOLD THE KNIFE AS HORIZONTAL AS IS PRACTICAL TO ENSURE A CLEAN CUT.

Cutting page edges

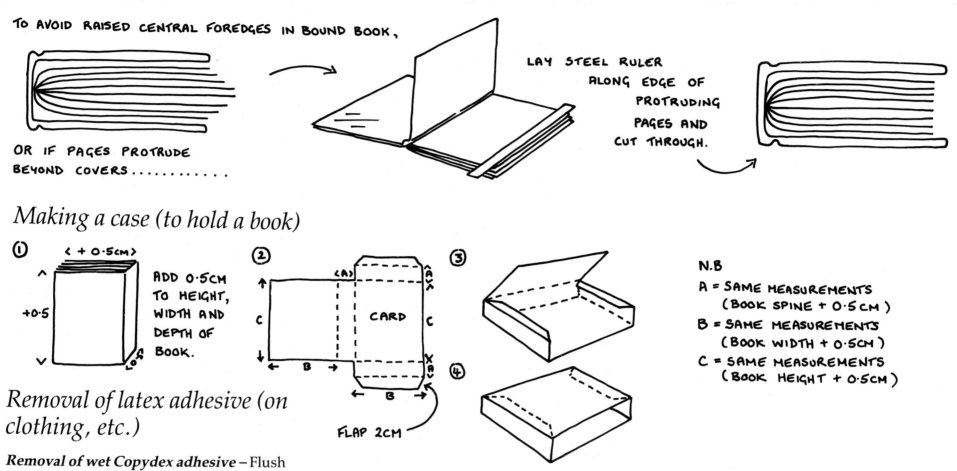

TO AVOID RAISED CENTRAL FOREDGES IN BOUND BOOK,

OR IF PAGES PROTRUDE BEYOND COVERS............

LAY STEEL RULER ALONG EDGE OF PROTRUDING PAGES AND CUT THROUGH.

Making a case (to hold a book)

① < + 0.5CM >
+0.5
ADD 0.5CM TO HEIGHT, WIDTH AND DEPTH OF BOOK.

② <A> CARD C B X A FLAP 2CM

③

④

N.B
A = SAME MEASUREMENTS (BOOK SPINE + 0.5 CM)
B = SAME MEASUREMENTS (BOOK WIDTH + 0.5 CM)
C = SAME MEASUREMENTS (BOOK HEIGHT + 0.5 CM)

Removal of latex adhesive (on clothing, etc.)

Removal of wet Copydex adhesive – Flush immediately with cold water.

Removal of dried Copydex adhesive – Remove bulk of adhesive then rub with pencil rubber. Any remaining adhesive should be softened using a proprietary liquid dry cleaner such as Dab-It-Off.

Appendix 2 – Equipment and suppliers

Knives
Cutters M18 (140 × 24 mm)
Blade replacements CB18
(wallets of ten blades).

Cutting mats
Expensive but virtually indestructable.
Small   CM30   (30 × 45 cm)
Medium CM45   (45 × 60 cm)
Large   CM60   (60 × 90 cm)
Catalogue and price list available from:
Edding (UK) Ltd, Merlin Centre, Acrewood
Way, St. Albans, Herts A14 0JY. (Tel: 0727
46688). Generous discounts to schools.

Steel rulers
30 cm safety rulers for small work and young
children, but 1 m for cutting A1/A2 paper.
Available from: Nottingham Educational
Supplies, Ludlow Hill Road, West Bridgford,
Nottingham NG2 6HD (Tel: 0602 452200). 1 m
rulers available from DIY shops.

Bookbinders' awls
Available from: Kutrite Ltd., Snow Lane,
Sheffield S3 7AL (Tel: 0742 739977). Minimum
order – seven awls.

Adhesives
Most adhesives e.g. PVA and latex (copydex)
are suitable for basic books. Available from
school's suppliers and DIY shops.

Bookbinders' needles and threads
Large darning needles available from
Nottingham Educational Supplies, and strong
thread available from good haberdashery
shops.

Coverboard
Available from Reeves Dryad, PO Box 38,
Leicester LE1 9BU (Tel: 0533 510405).
Greyboard – 635 × 762 mm, 1100/1725
microns. For local sources look under 'paper
and board manufacturers' in *Yellow Pages*.

Paper
Cheapest source probably your LEA Supplies
Department or Nottingham Educational
Supplies. Recommended 115/135 gsm
cartridge. SRA1 (640 × 900 mm) and SRA2
(450 × 640 mm). **NB** These sizes are slightly
larger than the A1, A2 measurements referred
to in this book but can be used,
proportionately in the same way, e.g. for A2
in the text read SRA2. (Alternatively, paper
can be cut down to A1, A2 sizes – A1 = 594 ×
841 mm; A2 = 420 × 594 mm.)

For wide range of papers including end of line
bargain offers and discount to schools contact:
R.K. Burt and Co., 57 Union Street, London
SE1 (Tel: 071-407 6474). Other suppliers
include:

Falkiner Fine Papers Ltd.,
76 Southampton Row, London WC1 B4AR
(tel: 071-831 1151). Wide range of papers
(including Japanese and marbled papers) and
bookbinding materials. Price lists and samples
available.

Paperchase, 213 Tottenham Court Road,
London W1P 9AF (tel: 071-580 8496).

One Nine Four, Unit 35 Union Mills,
Milnbridge, Huddersfield HD3 4NA
(Tel: 0484 460016).

Maureen Richardson, Romilly, Brilley, Hay on
Wye, Hereford HR3 6HE
(tel: 04973-546).
Send stamped addressed envelope for lists of
her beautiful handmade plant papers and
details of her paper making courses.

Weights of paper

gsm	IMP	(lb)	
100	50	Light weight	
130	62	Medium weight	
150	72		
190	90	Heavy weight	

Light/medium weight paper suitable for book
pages.
Medium/heavy weight suitable for covering
books and standing concertina books.

Developmental bookbinding

Bookbinding courses: London College of Printing, Elephant and Castle, London SE1 6SB run evening classes in basic bookbinding. Morley College, 61 Westminster Bridge, London SE1 7HT run part-time bookbinding courses.

For a list of bookbinding courses over the country contact: Designer bookbinders (Secretary), 6 Queens Square, London WC1N 3NR.

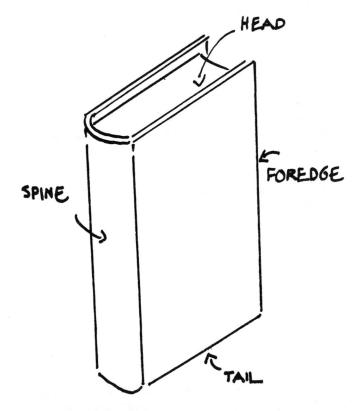

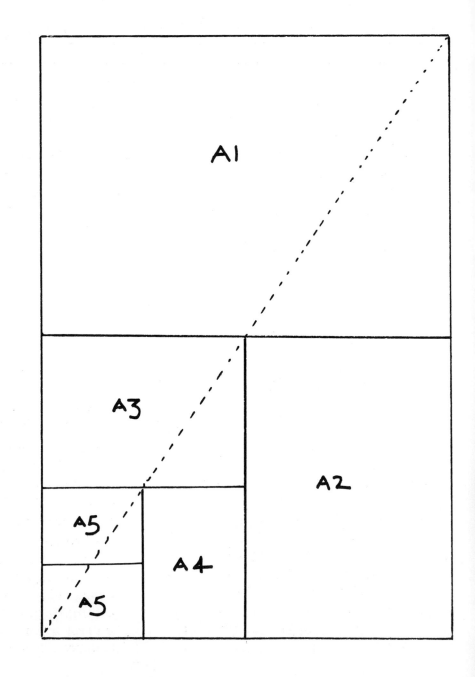

Appendix 3 – Useful books

Bookbinding
BENNETT, L. and SIMMONS, J. (1978) *Children Making Books*. A & C Black.
IKEGAMI, K. (1986) *Japanese Bookbinding*. Weatherhill New York; (available Crafts Council Shop, London).
JOHNSON, A.W. (1978) *Bookbinding*. Thames and Hudson.
JOHNSON, A.W. (1985) *Craft Bookbinding*. Thames and Hudson.
ROBINSON, I. (1984) *Introducing Bookbinding*. Oxford Polytechnic Press.

Lettering and design
GRISLIS, P. (1988) *The Calligraphy Book*. Ashton Scholastic.
HARVEY, M. (1985) *Creative Lettering*. The Bodley Head.
MANN, W. (1982) *Lettering and Lettering Display*. Van Nostrand Reinhold (paperback).
MORRIS, N. (1982) *The Lettering Book*. Ashton Scholastic.
PEARCE, C. (1982) *The Little Manual of Calligraphy*. Collins.
SASSOON, L. (1984) *The Practical Guide to Children's Handwriting*. Thames and Hudson.
SHEPHERD, M. (1984) *Learning Calligraphy*. Macdonald.
STRIBLEY, M. (1986) *The Calligraphy Source Book*. Macdonald.

VINCENT, C. (1986) *Lettering and Design*. Blandford Press.

Book illustration and decoration
LE HAMEL, C. (1986) *A History of Illuminated Manuscripts*. Guild Publications.
LEWIS, J. (1967) *The 20th Century Book*. Herbert.
ANON (1985) *Decorative Endpapers*. Victoria and Albert Colour Books Webb and Bower.

Books about children's books
ALDERSON, B. (1986) *Sing a Song for Sixpence*. Cambridge University Press.
AVERY, G. (1989) *Child' Eye*. Channel 4 Television.
BARR, J. (1986) *Illustrated Chidlren's Books*. The British library.
FEAVER, W. (1977) *When We Were Young*. Thames and Hudson.

Decorative bookbindings
FOOT, M. (1986) *Pictorial Bookbindings*. The British Library.
LEWIS, R.H. (1984) Fine Bookbinding in the Twentieth Century. David and Charles.

Miscellaneous
PINNELL (1986) *Village Heritage*. Alan Sutton. (A book produced by the children of Sopperton Church of England Primary School, Gloucestershire.)
THOMAS, A. (1975) *Great Books and Book Collectors*. Spring Books.

Children's Writing
ANDREW, M. (1989) *Language in Colour*. Belair.
BALAAM, J. and MERRICK, B. (1987) *Exploring Poetry 5–8*. National Association for the Teaching of English.
BEARD, R. (1984) *Children's Writing in the Primary School*. Hodder and Stoughton.
CALKINS, L. (1986) *The Art of Teaching Writing*. Heinemann.
HALL, N. (1987) *The Emergence of Literacy*. Hodder and Stoughton.
HALL, N. (1989) *Writing with Reason*. Hodder and Stoughton.
NEWMAN, J. (1984) *The Craft of Children's Writing*. Scholastic.
WRAY, D. (1987) *Bright Ideas Writing*. Scholastic.
ANON (1988) *Developing Children's Writing*. Scholastic.
ANON (1989) *Becoming a Writer*. (The Nelson National Writing Project.)